I0825322

The Baker's Percentage

MARA RIPANI

The Baker's Percentage

The simple formula for making perfect sourdough bread at home

Contents

PART 3
Core steps in depth

Preface

Too many passionate home bakers give up sourdough baking because they believe the process is inflexible.

There was only white, sliced bread being sold in the little town of Riverton, in South Australia, when my professional artist friend Lise moved there in the early 2000s. 'I'll have to learn to bake bread,' she said, and so she did. Over several years, I watched her pull loaf after loaf of sourdough from her Aga wood-fired oven between slapping lashings of paint on her canvases and managing multiple commitments, including children, exhibitions and artwork sales. 'I'll buy you a bread-baking book,' she offered one year for my birthday. She bought me *Wild Sourdough* by Yoke Mardewi. And that is when I too began to bake sourdough bread.

Once I began, I couldn't stop. It was addictive.

Sourdough bread became my kitchen companion, constantly exuding warmth and vivacity. No matter how tired I was, I always had enthusiasm for baking bread, and on nights when study kept me up late, knowing that I had leaven rising in the kitchen somehow made me feel like I wasn't alone.

How did Lise and I integrate sourdough making into our lives with such ease? By learning to use the Baker's Percentage – a really simple formula used by bakers all around the world to create, adapt and scale up or down recipes for breads and other doughs.

Most important for home bakers is that *the formula isn't fixed*. You can play with it – along with how you use the oven and fridge – to influence fermentation speed, leaving you free to bake whenever you want to, meaning you can pursue other adventures and responsibilities and make sourdough baking fit into any schedule.

When I set up Village Dreaming, my artisanal cooking school in Blampied, Victoria, and started teaching sourdough bread baking, I found that many participants had attended other sourdough classes or had read books by wonderful sourdough bakers but were still struggling to make bread in a domestic setting. Varying commitments to work, children and social lives got in the way.

Eventually, I realised that they had all learned what I call the 'utopian' method, a *singular* sourdough-baking pathway perfect for professional bakers and essential to running a bakery, but rarely practical in home baking.

In a bakery, there are hundreds of loaves of bread being made, using numerous flavours and flours, from fruit breads to pure white, wholemeal (whole-wheat) and wholegrain loaves. And they all need to be ready at the same time: when the bakery opens. The bakery shift, therefore, is planned to ensure that all the loaves are ready to bake at a similar time, with some minor staggering. For the day to run smoothly, factors like the strength of the leaven and the temperature of the room, leaven and water need to be tightly controlled. But for home bakers, making only a few loaves, there is much more flexibility.

In my cooking school I decided to focus on domestic baking, introducing my participants to the Baker's Percentage and the *multiple* pathways that can be taken to produce bread. As a home baker, you don't need to feed your leaven every day, nor do you need to discard any. You don't need to keep the leaven at a particular temperature, nor does your leaven need to always be at its prime before use. You have an enormous amount of wiggle room.

This book is for all the people who bought recipe books and signed up to sourdough-baking courses online during the pandemic lockdowns and then gave up because they thought there was only one way to make sourdough. The Baker's Percentage gives home bakers many pathways to baking their own sourdough. This book will help you to find the pathways that work for you.

How to use this book

SOURDOUGH BREAD IS NOT A CAKE
As you flick through this book, you will notice that it doesn't contain a lot of recipes. This is because sourdough bread is not a cake. While even a novice cake maker can follow a cake recipe and get the desired outcome, a novice sourdough baker needs to start with a good understanding of the bread-baking process to achieve success. That understanding will allow you to bake bread easily and with pure joy.

That's why I'm taking a different approach in this book from that of other recipe books. Instead of a big collection of recipes that follow a singular, step-by-step method with rigid instructions about factors like leaven temperature or freshness, forcing you to fit your life around baking, I am going to give you, above all, the *hows* and *whys* of sourdough bread baking.

This may sound a little daunting, and you may be thinking, 'Just give me a recipe and tell me exactly what to do.' But trust me: when you understand the process, you will be able to bake bread easily and, after some practice, instinctively. And you will find it possible to fit baking into your everyday schedule.

I'll show you how to use leaven regardless of its strength and acidity; how to incorporate dried seeds or fruit at the start, middle or end of the dough-making process; how to use the fridge to slow down fermentation when you are tired and want to go to bed; and how to reduce or increase sourness in your leaven or have it disappear altogether. I'll also explain the variations you can achieve by using diverse flours, due to their different protein (gluten) contents.

In addition, I'll introduce you to important sourdough terminology, so you'll understand why flour is called 'hard' or 'soft' and why the first fermentation is called the 'bulk fermentation', while the final fermentation is called the 'proof'. And I'm going to convince you that there are multiple ways to feed and manage a leaven. This is one of the most liberating bits of knowledge I can give you.

The book is designed to support existing sourdough recipe books by explaining each core step of the bread-baking process. There's a lot of information here, but it's organised in a way that starts you off with the basics, gets you baking, and then gives you extra knowledge as you need it, to refine and develop your bread and your bread-making process.

A LITTLE BIT ABOUT ME

I come from Le Marche, Italy, where the sea meets the mountains; a region gastronomically rich and diverse. I have the warmest of feelings in my heart when I think about my childhood there and the meals prepared. Rabbit cooked in a black olive sauce; sea snails in a rich, oily ragu and prised out of their shells with toothpicks; polenta spread on a large wooden board and erupting with pesto like a volcano. We ate goat roasted with rosemary; chestnuts baked and devoured like crisps; and, in autumn, soft, gooey persimmons.

I started Village Dreaming, my artisanal cooking school, because I love traditional food culture. Authentic meals always begin at the beginning, at the start of the food story. All the chapters are included, and the climax in the story is always reached just before you sit down to enjoy the meal.

These are the food stories I share at Village Dreaming. I want to begin at the beginning, with a walk through a sheep farm towards chestnut trees or to the kitchen garden. It's not just a cooking school but a big-hearted place where the kitchen is theatre and song, and where community can flourish.

Bread-baking tools

Your kitchen is most likely already stocked with equipment and tools that can be used to make sourdough bread – for example, scales, baking tins, bowls and knives. You can mix ingredients in any large bowl, use a soup bowl to hold dough after it has been shaped and bake bread in any greased baking tin. So don't feel any pressure to purchase new equipment.

However, if you plan to bake bread regularly, if and when possible, I highly recommend obtaining the equipment listed below in order of importance:

DIGITAL SCALES

Flat digital scales make weighing dough portions particularly easy when you're dividing the bulk. They also allow you to tare (bring the reading back to zero) after each ingredient is added, making it easier to discern the weights of individual ingredients.

TRANSPARENT, SQUARE OR RECTANGULAR PLASTIC FOOD CONTAINER

It should be large enough to hold multiple kilograms (or pounds) of dough, and the sides mustn't taper in any direction. These containers make it so much easier to measure the bulk fermentation rise.

PROFESSIONAL BREAD TINS

To bake the basic sourdough loaf on page 42, you'll need a 450 g (1 lb) capacity loaf tin. Its dimensions should be 10 cm (4 in) depth, 23.5 cm × 10.5 cm (9¼ in × 4¼ in) inside top and 22 cm × 9 cm (8¾ in × 3½ in) outside base. As you progress to different-sized loaves and baking loaves in batches, you'll soon be wanting more.

PROOFING BASKETS (BANNETONS)

These baskets are designed to hold doughs during proofing that are going to be baked as free-form loaves. They're strong and durable.

SCORING LAME

Made specifically for scoring (cutting) the surface of the dough, lames usually consist of a wooden or plastic handle with a razor blade attachment. My preferred lames use a razor blade and give you the option of placing that blade in a curved or flat position. For beginner bakers, a flat blade can be easier to handle.

DOUGH SCRAPER

Buy one of the silicone or plastic ones, as they bend and help you get every bit of dough out of the bowl.

FLAMEPROOF CASSEROLE DISH

Also known as a Dutch oven, these are heavy, lidded cast-iron or enamelled pots in which many people bake free-form loaves. They trap the moisture emitted from the dough, creating steam that helps the dough rise. They must be used with a very hot oven. There are several designs to choose from. The most suitable ones have a shallow skillet base, which allows you to put the dough inside safely when the casserole dish is hot.

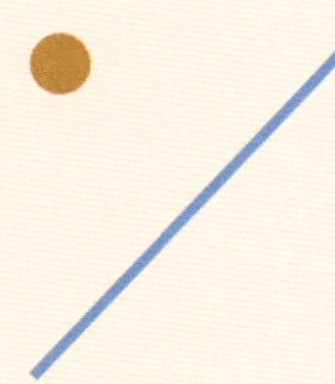

OVENS FOR BREAD BAKING

Not all ovens are the same, and some ovens are far better at baking bread than others. As home bakers, we generally need to work with the oven we already have. Most ovens will produce excellent tin loaves, and some (those that can get extremely hot) will produce excellent free-form loaves – that is, loaves baked without a tin or any other structural support.

Most modern ovens are fan-forced, which means they should be able to spread heat evenly across the oven chamber, but many don't. It's worth checking your oven's real temperature, with an oven thermometer, before you set out to make bread.

Some ovens (like mine) are supposed to be able to reach 250°C (475°F) but in fact can manage no more than 210°C (400°F), which is too low for free-form loaves and for using a flameproof casserole dish (Dutch oven). In these ovens, free-form loaves will achieve only moderate oven spring (the final part of the rise, which happens during baking). On the other hand, tin loaves will achieve a full oven spring in these ovens.

What domestic ovens lack that professional bakers' ovens have is thermal mass, which can absorb large amounts of heat and release it back towards the baking bread. Commercial ovens also trap humidity in the first 20 minutes of the bake – ideal for bread baking – while domestic ovens are designed to let humidity escape the oven chamber via a vent on the top of the oven door.

If you're looking for a new oven and want it to be good for bread baking, or if you happen to be thinking of setting up a micro-bakery at your home, make sure you investigate the size of any candidate's oven chamber, so you know how many loaves you can fit in at a time. In addition, the ideal oven will have the following features:

- **even temperature throughout the oven chamber or separate temperature controls for each oven deck**
- **excellent door seals**
- **thermally insulated, triple-glazed door**
- **integrated steam function**
- **capacity to reach a genuine 250°C (475°F) or above.**

Glossary

Here is a list of terms I use regularly in this book. Refer back to these pages to refresh your memory, if you're unsure what something means. Within time, these terms will become very familiar to you.

aerobic: processes or organisms that require oxygen

anaerobic: processes or organisms that do not require oxygen

autolyse: the process by which flour and water are mixed together and allowed to rest for a designated period of time, in the absence of salt and leaven, to allow gluten to develop before fermentation begins. This reduces the amount of overall kneading and can sometimes lead to a bread with better colour and flavour. Compare with fermentolyse.

bacteria: single-celled organisms

Baker's Percentage: a formula in which the individual weights of the salt, water, leaven and other ingredients used to make bread are expressed as percentages of the total flour weight, which is always expressed as 100%. It enables bakers to scale recipes up and down and to add or remove ingredients freely when developing recipes.

bench rest: a designated period of time during which dough is allowed to rest on a benchtop after preshaping, to further develop gluten

bread crumb: the internal texture of bread, which can be open, with large and small holes; or closed, with many fine, small holes

bulk fermentation: the first time the entire dough (the bulk) ferments

fermentation: the process caused by bacteria and yeast breaking down complex carbohydrates into simple sugars, producing acids, alcohol and gases

fermentolyse: the process by which flour, water and leaven (and, in this book, salt) are mixed together and allowed to rest for a designated period of time, during which fermentation begins. Compare with autolyse.

final shaping: the last time an individual bread dough is shaped before being placed in a tin or basket for proofing

free-form loaf: bread baked without a tin or any other structural support

gluten: a combination of two proteins, glutenin and gliadin, found in grains, which contributes elasticity, strength, viscosity and extensibility to dough

hard flour: flour with a high protein (gluten) content

hydration: water amount or proportion used in a bread recipe

kneading: stretching of dough to develop gluten

leaven: in this book, a mature flour ferment produced after fermentation has occurred in a starter and used for raising (expanding) bread dough before and during baking

preshaping: the shaping of individual bread doughs to test their structural strength and to further develop gluten before final shaping

proofing: the last time the dough is fermented, after division (if necessary) and before baking

scoring: cuts made to the surface of bread dough to allow it to fully expand during baking

shaping: the process in which dough is stretched and rolled in on itself to create surface tension and the desired loaf shape

soft flour: flour with a low protein (gluten) content

sourdough: a bread, also known as 'wild yeast bread' and 'naturally leavened bread', characterised by a distinct sour flavour (when desired)

starter: in this book, an immature flour ferment produced the very first time you mix flour and water together to cause the flour to ferment

wild yeast: yeasts naturally present on the surface of flour, and in the environment generally, and used to make sourdough bread

yeast: single-celled fungi capable of converting sugars into alcohol, carbon dioxide and acids

PART 1

Sourdough basics

Making sourdough bread can seem anything but basic at first, but it will become so, and in fact you will marvel at your capacity to fit sourdough baking into your already deliciously rich life. For the home baker, the humble bread tin and the simplest of ovens will see you baking beautiful, professional-looking loaves. When a little more adventure is called for and a challenge beckons, then free-form loaves will keep you on your toes.

CHAPTER 1

Homemade sourdough bread

The kitchen is theatre and song.

What is sourdough bread?

All breads are fermented, but some are fermented for longer than others, and that is true of sourdough bread. A basic loaf of sourdough bread is made from flour, water, salt and leaven and has a long fermentation time (up to 12 hours) compared to commercially made yeasted bread (two hours). It uses leaven to achieve this fermentation.

Leaven is a mixture of flour and water that looks like pancake batter. When flour and water are mixed together, the yeasts and bacteria that are naturally present on the surface of the flour begin fermentation with the help of an enzyme in the flour. The fermentation produces, among other things, carbon dioxide, making the bread rise; and lactic and acetic acids, giving the bread its signature flavours when desired.

Why eat sourdough bread?

An especially good reason for eating sourdough bread is that it tastes great. In addition, it has a beautiful chewy texture and a crunchy crust; it can be made into all types of loaves, from a sandwich loaf to a soup-slurping loaf; it has a long shelf life of over a week; and, finally, it is aesthetically beautiful. Some people make grandiose claims about how much better sourdough bread is for you than other types of breads. I am no expert and won't be addressing the subject here, except to remind you of one important aspect of any bread's health benefits: the amount of fibre it contains. It is well established that a diet high in fibre is essential for good digestive health. Wholegrain flour is made from the entire grain kernel, resulting in flour that is much higher in fibre than white flour. So, using wholegrain flour is vital for getting the most health benefits possible from your bread.

However, if your diet is currently low in fibre and has been low for many years, you should introduce higher quantities of fibre into your bread-making recipes slowly, over several months. Some people on low-fibre diets will experience digestive discomfort if high quantities of fibre are introduced too quickly.

Sourdough fermentation

The word 'fermentation' will be used a lot throughout this book, so it's important to understand what it means. Fermentation is a process by which food is changed chemically through the action of yeasts and bacteria to sometimes produce gases, heat, acids and ethanol, or a combination of these products, in either an anaerobic or an aerobic environment. In this book, we are interested in the fermentation of flour, an anaerobic process that turns complex carbohydrates into simple sugars and creates acids, ethanol and carbon dioxide.

Fermentation relies heavily on the presence of water, either in a solid-state form or in a freely available form. An example of solid-state fermentation is when soya beans are fermented to create tempeh, and yeasts and bacteria come to rely on the water present on the surface and interior of the solid beans to create that fermentation. On the other hand, a starter, leaven and dough all rely on the addition of water to catalyse fermentation in flour.

Freely available water is crucial to the fermentation of dough for several reasons. It allows ingredients (flour, salt and leaven) to combine and interact with each other. Also, it supports the activity of amylase – the enzyme that breaks down starch into sugars; gelatinises starches to create a glistening, chewy bread crumb; and, most importantly, supports bacterial and yeast activity responsible for producing carbon dioxide, lactic and acetic acids and ethanol.

Fermentation changes the flavours and textures of foods to create new flavours and textures greatly enjoyed by humans. Fresh food that contains a high content of water can be fermented to make it last longer. For example, cabbages are fermented in many parts of the world, including Korea (to create kimchi) and Germany (to create sauerkraut), meaning communities can continue eating cabbage when it isn't in season. Hundreds of foods are fermented, from vegetables, fruits and grains to cocoa beans, cheese, coffee beans, soya beans and meat, to name just a few.

In the case of sourdough bread, we are fermenting flour made from grains such as wheat and spelt, not to make it last longer but to change its flavour and to make it expand, rise and bubble when turned into dough. In the absence of water, that dry flour will keep well and does not need to be fermented to make it last longer. Our reason for fermenting it is to activate microbial activity, which produces carbon dioxide, which makes bread rise; lactic and acetic acids, which give sourdough its signature flavour (when desired) and act as preservatives; and ethanol (in small quantities), most of which evaporates during baking.

Why bake sourdough bread at home?

No one ever complains that they have a bread-baking housemate. Bread is a deeply loved food, and it's very likely you will be deeply loved for making it.

Making your own sourdough gives you an affordable way to eat high-quality bread. An artisanal sourdough loaf is expensive to buy ready-made – a reflection of all the work that goes into making it and the fact that it weighs twice as much as commercially produced sliced bread. For a similar cost, you can easily make three large loaves at home.

Bread is known as a 'dietary staple', which means it's a commonly eaten food and comprises a large part of a household's diet, as well as its energy and nutrient intake. This is why baking bread at home is a powerful act: you can play a part in improving the health of all who live with you, by ensuring that the bread they eat includes a high percentage of wholegrain flour – and that it excludes a host of unhealthy additives.

Commercial bread commonly contains a combination of the ingredients listed below, added not to improve human health but to deal with issues that arise from mass production or to create particularly soft bread:

- preservatives (e.g., calcium propionates) that allow bakeries to pack bread in plastic bags while it is still hot
- oil or fat to make the bread softer
- distarch phosphate to give the bread crumb a smooth, velvety feel

- emulsifiers (e.g., lecithin, mono- and diglycerides) to ensure the oil or fat doesn't separate from the water component of the dough and to increase shelf life and the bread's softness
- bleaching agents (e.g., benzoyl peroxide, chlorine dioxide) to increase the bread's whiteness and softness
- food colouring made from vegetables and fruits or caramel to make white bread look like wholegrain bread
- maturing agents (e.g., chlorine dioxide, ammonium persulfate) to speed up the bread-making process, make the bread look bright white and increase the bread's softness
- guar gum to soften the bread.

In addition, some ingredients are commonly added to commercial bread in an attempt to improve human health. Many Western governments have mandated that bread, due to its being a dietary staple, must include a range of added vitamins and minerals to help prevent a few of the many debilitating disorders that occur in the absence of a well-balanced diet. The three main beneficial additives in bread are iodine (a mineral), folic acid (vitamin B9) and thiamine (vitamin B1).

However, it's possible to get your required daily dose of these from eating a balanced diet, meaning there's no need for home bakers to add them to their bread. For example, iodine is present in fish, seaweed, milk and iodised salt; thiamine is found in meat, fish and whole grains; and folic acid occurs in green leafy vegetables, beans, fresh fruits, peanuts and eggs.

As well as leaving out unnecessary ingredients, baking your own bread allows you to include ingredients and ingredient combinations according to your own needs and preferences. You can create bespoke breads using grains such as spelt, emmer, Khorasan wheat and rye. You can make low-salt or no-salt breads. You can make breads containing your favourite nuts and seeds, or with onion, garlic, cheese, pumpkin, beetroot (beet), dill, chives, berries, fruits or even chocolate. The options are endless.

I believe that making your own bread is important because it teaches you a new skill and a new language, which is deeply enriching; and it helps to build community. If we let commercial industries do all the work for us, where will our stories grow from? We can't build personal stories through the work of strangers.

I have found that life is about building knowledge, experience and community and is never a hack, trick or secret. I encourage you to find others who are baking, and hold informal gatherings where you live, to share and gain knowledge, to build friendships.

This book is dedicated to home bakers, people who are making bread while surrounded by a multitude of distractions and requests that interrupt baking: young family members who want to be dropped off at friends' houses at short notice, friends who kindly send last-minute dinner invitations, housemates who also need access to the oven. The book favours the building of knowledge that will allow you flexibility when a bake can't go from A to Z without interruptions. Crucially, it favours the use of medium-strength or weak leaven, leaven that is flat, last fed a week or two ago, when you have no time for a fresh feed before a bake. It will show you different ways to manage leaven and approaches that will allow you to bake for decades. That is the motivation here.

You will often hear the word 'artisan' used in relation to sourdough baking. I think you will come to truly appreciate why after giving sourdough baking a go yourself.

Sourdough bread making is a rare, valuable skill. There are aspects to it that take practice, time and patience. You are likely to experience failures along the way. But stick with it.

This book offers you the most reliable method for long-term success. You're on the way to becoming an artisan. And while some may scoff at the word 'artisan' and think it ostentatious, you will have a little more insight as you begin to realise that it is a word that celebrates skills and knowledge gained in a very concerted way.

MICRO-BAKERIES

I'm in love with micro-bakeries. These are bakeries often established in people's homes. I love them because they build local communities.

Outside these homes you will find shelves full of sourdough breads of all kinds for sale, as well as cakes and biscuits. All over the world, locals are traipsing along garden paths to pick up bread from a baker they know well. The deep connections created in these places are truly beautiful.

Look for a mentor if you want to set up a micro-bakery, and volunteer to help them in exchange for their guidance. People who bake for a living work remarkably hard, as baking is both physically and intellectually demanding. So go out of your way, if you can, to offer meaningful help in exchange for their experiences and learnings.

CHAPTER 2

Key ingredients

The four key ingredients in sourdough bread are flour, water, salt and leaven.

Flour

For this part of the book, you're going to be working with two easy-to-use flours: for your starter and leaven, you'll be using wholemeal (whole-wheat) flour, and for your first loaf, you'll want high-protein (12–12.3%) white bread flour. To find out the protein content of your flour, first look at the nutrition content list on the bag. If you can't see it there, try the company's website or call them directly. In my experience, they will be very happy to tell you.

For more information on flour, see pages 66 and 96.

Water

Water is an essential ingredient in bread making and key to catalysing fermentation. Water also turns flour into dough and during baking causes the gelatinisation of starch granules to create a soft, chewy bread texture.

For information on sourdough hydration, see Chapter 6.

Salt

Salt aids in the development of the dough by tightening and strengthening gluten structure and adds necessary flavouring.

For information on using salt in sourdough, see page 102.

Leaven

At this point, you may be wondering why yeast isn't listed above as a key ingredient. Have you ever heard sourdough bread called 'wild yeast bread' or 'naturally leavened bread'? All these terms refer to the same type of bread, and they inform you that the bread isn't made using commercial yeast that comes in a packet (dried or activated) or fresh from a deli. Instead, the bread makes use of the yeasts (and bacteria) that are naturally present on flour. These wild yeasts are cultivated in a leaven, which ferments the dough; in turn, this fermentation makes the bread rise (see Chapter 3).

WILD YEAST VERSUS COMMERCIAL YEAST

You may have seen a meme during the pandemic that said, 'Am I the only one not making sourdough bread?' It appeared when people were being forced to stay at home, and it highlighted just how many people wanted to learn to bake bread. And not just any bread: they wanted to make sourdough bread. I suspect the reason for this was that, in a world where everything is made for us, and with so many of us working mostly with keyboards and screens, the adventure of making something from scratch felt truly marvellous.

Yeasts are types of fungi formed from single cells. They occur naturally in the environment and are all around us. When we talk about 'wild yeast' in sourdough baking, we are referring to yeasts that come from our environment. The flour we use is naturally coated in the yeasts (and bacteria) we need to make bread. This is why all starter recipes – including the one in this book – ask you to simply mix flour with water.

For thousands of years, humans have relied on wild yeast to produce fermented foods like cheese, alcohol, cured meats, preserved vegetables, coffee, chocolate and bread. Then, in the 1800s, yeast became available to purchase. The yeast species used by bread makers that is sold as 'dried yeast' is called *Saccharomyces cerevisiae*. It was originally harvested from soil and trees. That yeast is now produced in factories; it is allowed to multiply and reproduce in large fermenting vats before being dried and sold. From the many yeast species that are suitable for making bread, this one was favoured by the scientific manufacturing community thanks to its effectiveness, fermentation speed and ease of reproduction under lab conditions.

The fascinating process of commercial yeast making is long and complicated, requires huge pieces of equipment, is extremely energy intensive and produces vast amounts of waste (which should not be taken lightly in the context of climate change). So why would anyone choose to buy this dried yeast, when wild yeasts are naturally occurring, readily available and free? Well, you know the answer: life feels a little less hard when you can subcontract work to someone else. Humans are also fascinated with finding easier ways of doing things, and dried yeast does make for an easier way of producing bread at home.

However, wild yeast bread with long fermentation times produces complex, delicious flavours, from acetic and lactic acids, that can't be attained from dried yeast and short fermentations. The wild yeasts also naturally preserve bread in ways that are not harmful to human health, make bread last longer (if properly stored) and can help some people better digest the bread grain used.

But also, I can't emphasise enough the huge pleasure to be gained from the new skills, new language and rituals that come from baking wild yeast bread and from the community you will build making it. And if you combine wild yeast bread making with the use of predominantly wholegrain flours, you will be making bread that is extremely healthy – a rare product in today's world.

CHAPTER 3

Make your starter & leaven

When you first make a starter, your aims are to activate then strengthen fermentation.

Starter basics

WHAT IS A STARTER?

A starter is a thick, pancake-like batter made from flour and water. As we saw in Chapter 1, once flour becomes wet, it begins to ferment. The starter's temperature affects how quickly this happens: warm temperatures speed up fermentation, and cold temperatures slow down fermentation. Only the freezer puts a complete halt on fermentation.

MAKING YOUR OWN STARTER

When you first make your own starter, there are two distinct objectives:

1. Activate the fermentation: this happens as soon as you mix the flour and water. Easy.

2. Strengthen the fermentation: discard (remove) some starter and feed (add fresh flour and water to) the remaining starter until it can double in height in four hours.

STARTER AND LEAVEN TERMINOLOGY

When you enter the world of sourdough baking, you will hear many terms used to describe a flour ferment, including biga, leaven, levain, madre bianca, mother, pâte fermentée, poolish, preferment, sourdough starter, sponge and starter.

To keep things straightforward, throughout this book, I use two words to describe the two stages of a flour ferment:

- **STARTER: an *immature* flour ferment, produced the *very first time* you mix flour and water together to cause the flour to ferment**

- **LEAVEN: a *mature* flour ferment, produced after fermentation has occurred in a starter.**

When making a starter, it's essential to discard some of it before feeding it, as you'll be feeding the starter twice a day. The twice-daily feeds are done to build fermentation strength, speed and reliability, and these properties in a starter are achieved if there is more fresh flour in the starter than old flour.

By 'old' flour, I mean flour that has been fermenting for too long and is of little use to yeasts and bacteria because they can't eat it (ferment it) – since they already have. If they can't ferment it, no more carbon dioxide can be made. Only new flour being added can produce a new batch of carbon dioxide.

The old flour will also contain acids and ethanol, as these are by-products of the fermentation process. The greater the amount of old flour in the starter, the greater the amount of acid and ethanol present. If a starter is allowed to become very acidic with high amounts of ethanol, it will negate your chances of producing a speedy, strong and reliable starter (leaven), and the starter will end up containing highly degraded gluten, as high acidity and ethanol break down gluten structure. You would also need a very large jar to store the twice daily feeds.

It's vital to understand that these regular discards and feeds are important when *making* a starter, but that once the starter has proven its strength and matured into a leaven, you have the option of *never* discarding.

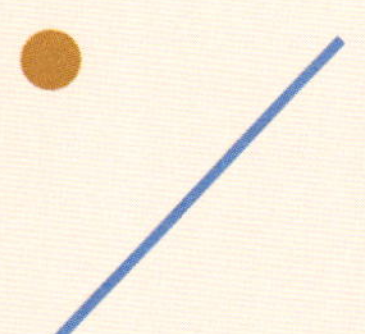

THE STARTER LIFE CYCLE

You can see when a starter is fermenting, because over several hours it will rise; that is, it will increase in volume. When it reaches its maximum height, it will then fall again.

Every time you remove some of the starter and follow this with an addition of fresh flour and water to the remaining starter, the starter will rise, reach maximum height, then fall down again. This is what you should expect: rise and fall, rise and fall.

Starter

You're ready to make your first starter. A quick reminder: always clean your hands and tools thoroughly before making and caring for your starter.

YOU WILL NEED

1 × 1 litre (34 oz) jar (it can be bigger but not smaller) with a wide opening and lid
sticky labels (or masking tape) and pen
2 rubber bands (big enough to fit around the jar)
100 g (3.5 oz) wholemeal (whole-wheat) flour, plus at least 2 kg (70.5 oz) for feeding
100 g (3.5 oz) water, plus at least 2 kg (70.5 oz) for feeding
food thermometer

1. Prepare the jar

Wash the jar in *hot*, soapy water, rinse it with hot water and allow it to air dry.

Next, weigh the jar on kitchen scales. Write the weight and today's date on a sticky label or masking tape and stick it onto the side of the jar. This will allow you to work out at the end of the process how much starter you made and how many days it took for the starter to mature into a strong leaven.

Stretch the rubber bands to fit around the body of the jar; you'll be using them later.

2. Mix flour and water together in the jar

Spoon the flour into the jar, then heat the water to 35°C (95°F) (use a food thermometer) and pour it into the jar.

Using a spatula long enough to reach the bottom of the jar, mix the flour and water together really well, until there are no patches of dry flour. Look round the bottom and side of the jar to make sure all the flour is wet.

At this stage, the starter will be very thick, with a mousse-like consistency. Smell your starter and take note of the fragrance: it will smell like wet flour – nothing more.

With a knife, scrape all the starter off the spatula and into the jar.

Give the spatula a wash, and while it's wet, use it to push down any starter clinging to the side of the jar. Wet the spatula as many times as necessary to produce a clean line at the top of the starter. This is to prevent patches of leaven from drying out and forming crusts on the side of the jar.

You will now have a clean jar with a clear leaven height. Place the lid on the jar, simply to keep dust and insects out; it doesn't need to be secured.

3. Mark the top of the starter

Move both rubber bands that you earlier put around the jar so that they sit at the same level as the top of the starter.

Later in the process, when the starter begins to rise (see opposite), use one of the rubber bands to follow the top of the starter, moving it whenever the starter moves. From this, you will be able to see where the starter reaches in height once maximum fermentation has taken place compared to its starting point, marked by the stationary rubber band.

4. Wait for fermentation to begin and to progress

The starter will begin fermenting if it's kept in a warm environment. If your ambient air temperature is below 25°C (75°F), place the jar in your oven on the top shelf and keep it warm by putting a tray of boiling water on the floor of the oven. (Put a note on the oven door warning everyone in your house that you have leaven inside.)

After one day, you should detect some small bubbles either at the top or throughout the starter, showing fermentation has taken place. At temperatures below 25°C (75°F) it may take two days, so use the oven method to keep it warm.

By the second day, if you kept your starter warm, you should begin to see large bubbles in it. At this point, try smelling it again. Does it smell different? A little bit yeasty and funky?

If you're not sure whether the bubbles are large or whether it smells yeasty, wait a bit longer. Leave the starter in the warmth of the oven (add freshly boiling water to the tray) and keep observing. You want large bubbles and a yeasty fragrance, but that yeasty smell shouldn't get too strong.

The starter will not have risen at this stage; therefore, we're not looking for a rise yet, only small and then large bubbles.

5. Feed the starter

As soon as the starter is producing large bubbles and has a definite yeasty fragrance, it's time to feed it. (As stated, the first feed should occur after around one or two days.)

Keep 50 g (1.76 oz) of the starter and discard the rest (or keep the discarded portion for making something else).

For leaven discard recipes, see Part 4.

Spoon in 100 g (3.5 oz) wholemeal flour, then heat 100 g (3.5 oz) water to 35°C (95°F) and pour it into the jar.

Now repeat what you did in step 2, making sure to combine the remaining starter with the fresh ingredients, and clean the side of the jar with the wet spatula.

Finally, mark the top of the starter with both rubber bands.

6. Feed the starter until it doubles in volume in four hours

Continue to keep the starter in a warm place and observe it regularly. Use one of the rubber bands to follow its rise and fall as its bubbles fill and deflate.

When the starter has doubled in volume (about ten hours after the first feed), and after the bubbles start to deflate, it's time for the second feed. Follow the feeding instructions given in step 5. From here on, always feed the starter only after the bubbles begin to deflate.

Continue to feed the starter in this way each time it doubles in volume and then deflates. It will gradually ferment faster and faster. You should see a huge increase in starter volume after you feed it (a doubling or almost a tripling) and observe notes of acidity or sourness.

Keep feeding the starter for as many days as it takes for it to double in volume in four hours – this point can take up to two weeks to reach. (If two weeks feels too long to wait, you can use the leaven sooner, before it has become strong.)

When the starter is doubling reliably within four hours of being fed, you have yourself a strong leaven. Happiness.

For instructions on caring for your leaven, see page 35.

Leaven basics

WHAT IS LEAVEN?

Leaven is used as an ingredient in sourdough bread: it makes fermentation occur in the dough, and the fermentation makes the bread rise. As we have seen, leaven is a mature starter. The word 'mature' here means that the leaven ferments and doubles in volume reliably and promptly after it has been fed compared to a starter. While a starter takes up to 24 hours to *begin* fermentation, a leaven responds to feeding very quickly.

In fact, leaven has the capacity to ferment and double in volume within four hours of being fed. When a leaven ferments at this speed, we call it a 'strong' leaven.

As with the starter, temperature affects the speed at which leaven ferments and increases in volume. Warm temperatures speed up fermentation, and cooler temperatures slow it down. This is important to know, so that you don't think your leaven is failing if it doesn't ferment at the same speed every time.

For more information about leaven fermentation speed, see page 88.

HOW IS LEAVEN USED TO MAKE BREAD RISE?

Fermentation and rising occur in bread dough when we use leaven as an ingredient. Yeasts and bacteria present in the leaven act as leavening agents; that is, they produce carbon dioxide when they break down carbohydrates in flour into simple sugars, and it's this carbon dioxide that leavens bread. The process goes like this: you take out a portion of leaven from the leaven jar, leaving a little bit behind to be sure you have some for your next loaf. You put the leaven portion in the bowl where your bread dough will be made. To that leaven you add water, flour and salt, mix the ingredients well and then allow them to rest.

The yeasts and bacteria in your leaven now have access to more wet flour, so fermentation can again take place. This time, though, the fermentation is occurring in the bowl: in the dough.

Over many hours, the yeasts and bacteria introduced into the dough by your leaven will release those key products of carbon dioxide and lactic and acetic acids as they break down the flour.

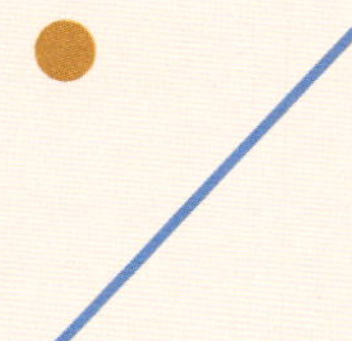

USE CLEAN HANDS AND TOOLS

To keep your leaven healthy, use clean hands and tools every time you touch it. And if you're handling your phone during leaven making, wash your hands after each phone use: your phone is the dirtiest tool in your kitchen.

Caring for your leaven

You have completed feeding your starter and have kept it warm. Once it is doubling reliably, you have a leaven. If it is doubling in volume within four hours of feeding, you have a strong leaven. That leaven will need to be cared for and managed. Remember: always clean your hands and tools before caring for your leaven.

WEIGHING YOUR LEAVEN

You can weigh your leaven to find out how much you have made. Remember that you noted the weight of the empty jar on the sticky label or masking tape stuck to the jar. Now place the leaven jar containing the leaven on a set of scales and weigh it. Calculate the leaven weight using this equation:

total weight of jar and leaven
– weight of empty jar
= weight of leaven

STORING YOUR LEAVEN

You can begin using your leaven to make bread as soon as it starts to ferment reliably. Alternatively, put it in the fridge until you need it.

If you think you won't get a chance to use it for several weeks, after it has been in the fridge for one week, discard and feed it using the same flour and water weights that were given in step 5 of the starter recipe: 100 g (3.5 oz) flour and 100 g (3.5 oz) water. This time, use cold water to slow down fermentation and then put it back in the fridge. Repeat this once every week if, after making your leaven, you don't get a chance to use it.

These additional discards and feeds are important for a recently made leaven that isn't being used, because the leaven lacks sourness, and a lack of sourness in a recently made leaven can sometimes lead to mould growth.

If the leaven becomes very funky from being left in the fridge unfed for too long, simply discard all but a teaspoon's worth and feed it using the same flour and water weights as when you first made the starter: 100 g (3.5 oz) flour and 100 g (3.5 oz) cold water. Then place it back in the fridge once more.

When you plan to use the leaven, leave it at room temperature after a feed and use it once it has completed its fermentation – that is, when it has risen as far as it can and is on its way down.

MANAGING YOUR LEAVEN

The speed at which leaven ferments and doubles in volume – also called its 'strength' – can be controlled and varied. Leaven can be described as 'strong', 'medium' and 'weak'. A weak leaven takes much longer than a strong leaven to ferment and double in volume. When leaven is used to make bread, its strength affects the speed at which the bread dough rises, determining the overall time needed to make a loaf.

As we have seen, at a doubling rate of four hours, a leaven is described as 'strong', at its peak, and it's the type of leaven used in bakeries – and called for in many sourdough recipe books and websites. Crucially, to make a strong leaven, many bakers are led to believe that they need to feed it twice a day, and even up to three times a day.

It is at this point that many home bakers' enthusiasm for sourdough baking gets wobbly. Their schedule doesn't allow for a twice-daily session of leaven care. They feel uncomfortable about throwing away so much leaven, but they don't have time to bake – or the capacity to eat – pancakes or cakes to use it up. The cost of the flour needed to keep up so much feeding is daunting. It seems too hard.

But you need to know that you can make great bread (tin bread and free-form bread) by working with a leaven that takes longer – much longer – than four hours to ferment and double in volume. As a home baker, you're not restricted to a commercial bakery's schedule, and you can be super-flexible with how you manage your leaven and with the strength of your leaven.

By this I mean that if you're using a medium-strength leaven – for example, one that you last fed a week ago – you'll know that the dough will take maybe six hours instead of four hours to complete its first rise. So, you can just use that time to get on with your work, or pick up friends from the airport, or go to the gym, knowing that the dough will be rising slowly.

I have baked excellent bread with leaven that was so weak that it smelled like blue-vein cheese (but was mould free), just to prove the point.

For more information about managing leaven fermentation speed, see page 92.

GIFTED LEAVEN

It's a very beautiful thing to receive leaven as a gift or to use leaven handed down through generations. The stories that come with gifted leaven are important; they connect you through time with the people you love or with new friends.

Gifted leaven will be neither better nor worse than your own homemade leaven in terms of its performance as a leavening agent. It is, however, a jar full of handed-down memories.

In most cases, people gift leavens instead of starters. However, regardless of whether you've been given a starter or a leaven, you will need to ask the giver when it was last fed. You want to know whether the starter or leaven completed its fermentation after its last feed, so that you can work out when to feed it next. In other words, did it rise as high as it could and now is on its way down? Or is it still rising?

A feed is always done after the yeasts and bacteria in the leaven have finished feasting. If the leaven is rising – showing the feasting is still happening – there's no need to put extra food on the microscopic table, as it will make it impossible for you to know when to use the leaven to make bread. Instead, you need to feed it anytime from the moment it reaches full fermentation height to the moment it crashes all the way back down.

Once you know when to next feed the leaven, test its fermentation speed. If that speed is slow and you want to make it fast, feed it regularly, straight after fermentation has finished. Or, if you're only baking once a week, slow down the fermentation by reducing the number of feeds. Essentially, you can develop a feeding schedule to match your baking schedule: once a day, once a week, or once a month – and anything in between.

THE 13 CORE STEPS OF BREAD BAKING

1

Prepare a leaven

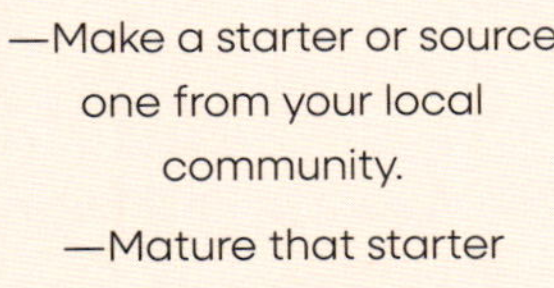

—Make a starter or source one from your local community.

—Mature that starter into a leaven.

To learn more, see page 82.

2

Mix the ingredients

—Add water, leaven, salt, flour in this order into a large bowl.

—Mix really well until it forms a dough with no patches of dry flour visible.

To learn more, see page 96.

3

Rest the dough

—Cover the dough in the bowl and let it rest for 30 minutes.

To learn more, see page 108.

4

Feed your leaven

—Add fresh flour and water to your leaven.

—Mix well, then scrape clean the inside of the jar to the top of the leaven.

—Put the leaven in the fridge.

To learn more, see page 112.

5

Knead the dough

—Knead the dough to develop gluten.

—Knead in one long session, or several shorter sessions interspersed with bench rests, until the dough is smooth and peels away easily from the surface.

To learn more, see page 116.

6

Bulk ferment the dough

—Transfer the dough to a greased container and seal the container.

—Leave until the dough has risen by one-third.

To learn more, see page 130.

7 Divide the dough

—If you're making more than one loaf, divide the dough into the number of portions required and ensure they are of equal weights.

To learn more, see page 136.

8 Preshape the dough

—Preshape the dough to check gluten strength.

If the dough is weak and barely holds its shape after a 15-minute rest, preshape it more than once.

To learn more, see page 138.

9 Final shape the dough

—Shape the dough according to the shape and size of the tin or proofing basket (banneton) you're using.

To learn more, see page 142.

10 Transfer the dough

—Place the shaped dough into a prepared tin or proofing basket (banneton).

To learn more, see page 148.

11 Proof the dough

—Leave the dough until it has risen to about 90% of its maximum potential and springs back slowly when you do a poke test.

—Preheat the oven to 250°C (475°F) fan-forced.

To learn more, see page 154.

12 Bake the bread

—If you're using a proofing basket (banneton), transfer the dough to a baking sheet, baking stone or a flameproof casserole dish (Dutch oven).

—Put the tin, baking sheet, stone or casserole dish on a high shelf in the preheated oven.

—Bake the bread for 30–40 minutes or until it is evenly golden brown and sounds hollow when tapped with a knuckle, or until it has an internal temperature of 95°C (203°F).

To learn more, see page 162.

13 Cool the bread

—Remove the loaf from the oven and immediately transfer to a cooling rack.

—Allow the loaf to cool completely before slicing.

To learn more, see page 166.

CHAPTER 4

Make your first loaf

There's nothing like practical experience. As a beginner, stick to making the same dough over and over again. Really get to know your dough.

Bread-baking basics

Let's get baking. This stage of the book is especially important if you are new to sourdough bread making. There's nothing like practical experience to back up the information you've already read and to help you understand all that's to come in the next part of the book. If you have already baked a few loaves and you're not ready to start baking just now, I'd encourage you to read this chapter anyway, to refresh your memory of the processes involved.

The recipe method in this chapter follows the 13 core steps outlined on pages 38–9 that all sourdough bakers take to make their bread. In this chapter, I'll lead you through each step. This is part of the hows of sourdough bread making. We'll examine the core steps in much more detail, including variations to them – the *whys* – in Part 3. You don't need to understand the whys to complete this stage, but if you have a question, turn to the corresponding step in Part 3, and you're likely to find the answer.

Before you start

For your first loaf, you're going to need leaven that has done a full fermentation – in other words, it has risen as far as it can go and is either on its way down or is already all the way down. A leaven that was last refreshed within the past week is fine, but if you notice a layer of dark liquid on its surface, this will be a build-up of ethanol, which you need to deal with before using it.
For information about ethanol build-up, see page 84.

To make your first loaf, set aside a day for baking. Even though you won't be actively baking for the entire time, you'll need to be available to see each step through. Allocate, say, from 9 am to 5 pm if you're in a fairly warm environment of around 20°C (70°F) or above, and longer if your environment is cooler.

Note that steps 7 and 8 in the basic sourdough loaf recipe on page 47 are core steps in sourdough baking, so they're briefly described. But they're only needed when you're making more than one loaf (step 7) and/or when you're baking a free-form loaf (step 8). When you're making your first loaf, you can skip these steps: after finishing step 6, go straight to step 9.

Basic sourdough loaf

YOU WILL NEED

- 1 × 450 g (1 lb) capacity bread tin
- 1 × 1.9 litre (4 pint) transparent, square or rectangular plastic food container with lid

---

- 408 g (14.39 oz) water, at room temperature
- 120 g (4.23 oz) wholemeal (whole-wheat) leaven
- 12 g (0.42 oz) non-iodised salt
- 600 g (21 oz) high-protein white bread flour
- 100 g (3.5 oz) wholemeal (whole-wheat) flour, for feeding leaven
- 100 g (3.5 oz) water, for feeding leaven

1

Prepare a leaven

If you've followed the starter recipe and caring for your leaven sections in the previous chapter, you've already completed this step. Just remember to remove your leaven from the fridge one hour before you plan to use it.

To learn more about starters and leavens, see Chapter 3.

Mix the ingredients

Add to a large bowl, in this order, the water, leaven, salt and bread flour. With one hand, mix the ingredients extremely well, using the other hand to hold and turn the bowl. Squish the dough in the mixing hand as if you are wringing a cleaning sponge. The aim here is to wet all the flour and to thoroughly combine all the ingredients. If you see small areas of dry flour, continue mixing. It's better to overmix than undermix, so give this a good five minutes of your time.

Flip the dough mass upside down to see if there are any dry patches of flour on the bottom or stuck to the bowl. If there are, mix them into the dough mass.

Keep looking and mixing until you're confident that every bit of flour is wet.

Then, with your clean hand, use a dough scraper (or another utensil) to remove all the dough from your mixing hand and push down any flaky bits of dough from the edge of the bowl, integrating them into the dough mass.

Now, with the hand you used to mix the dough, slip your fingers beneath the dough on the side furthest from you and stretch that side upwards until it breaks away from the rest of the dough. How quickly or at what point did it break? Observe the way the dough looks. Is it smooth or rough? Try to remember these points, as you'll refer back to them later.

Use your scraper to remove any remaining dough from your mixing hand and return it to the dough mass.

To learn more about mixing ingredients, see page 96.

3 Rest the dough

When all the flour in the dough looks wet, it's time for it to rest. Using a wet tea towel, a large plate or an inverted bowl, completely cover the top of the bowl containing the dough. Let the dough rest, covered like this, for 30 minutes.

To learn more about resting the dough, see page 108.

4 Feed your leaven

As the dough rests, you can feed your leaven. To your leaven jar, add the wholemeal flour and remaining water (cold), as you did when you fed the starter (page 33).

Using a small spatula, mix everything together in the jar. Then wet the spatula and use it to push down bits of leaven from the side of the jar to create a clear top line to the leaven – just as you did when you first made your starter.

Place your well-mixed leaven in the fridge, where it will ferment very slowly until your next bake.

To learn more about feeding your leaven, see page 112.

5 Knead the dough

FIRST KNEAD

When the dough has been resting for 30 minutes, using one hand, slip your fingers beneath the dough on the side furthest from you and stretch it upwards until it breaks, like you did earlier. Did you notice a difference? This time, the dough won't have broken as easily and will have stretched further before breaking.

Now take a good look at the dough. Does it look different from how it looked earlier? It should look smoother.

Okay, it's time to knead. The purpose of kneading (stretching) the dough is to develop its elasticity and eventually give the bread its structure.

There are lots of different kneading techniques to choose from, depending on your own preference or on the type of bread being made. For this first loaf, I recommend you use the stretch-and-fold method. It's super simple and does the job perfectly.

For this loaf, which needs less kneading than a free-form loaf, stretch and fold ten times, rotating the bowl after each stretch and fold. You're aiming for the dough to become smooth and shiny, able to stretch but also to hold its shape. It should sit away from the side of the bowl. Cover the dough once more and let it rest for 15 minutes.

To learn more about the stretch-and-fold method, see page 121.

SECOND KNEAD

Repeat exactly what you did for the first knead: stretch and fold the dough ten times, rotating the bowl after each stretch and fold.

If the dough is looking a bit rough after this knead, give it a further ten stretch and folds. It should look smooth by the end of this step.

To learn more about kneading, see page 116.

6

Bulk ferment the dough

It's time for the first fermentation, in which all the dough (the bulk) is kept as a single mass.

Lightly grease the interior base and sides of your food container with a teaspoon of oil. Any mild-flavoured vegetable oil will be fine for this – I normally use olive oil. This will make getting the dough back out of the container easier.

Scoop your dough from the bowl and into the container and, with wet fingers, push it down so that there are no gaps between the container and the dough and a roughly even surface is created. This will help you discern the dough's height.

Bending down to make sure your eyes are level with the height of the dough in the container, stick a piece of masking tape onto the outside of the container to mark the level of the top of the dough.

Seal the container with its lid and leave the dough for three hours.

After three hours, have a look at your dough as it sits in the container. Has it risen above the tape line? Can you see bubbles throughout the dough? Does it look lofty and bouncy?

The bulk fermentation is complete when the dough has risen by one-third of its original height. I don't expect it to have risen by that much after three hours, but it's good for you to observe it regularly. Wait until the dough has clearly risen by one-third before heading to the next step, no matter how long that takes. (If you happen to allow the dough to rise more than one-third, just move on to the next step as soon as you can.)

The speed at which dough ferments varies according to ambient air temperature and leaven strength. The bulk fermentation can take anywhere from four to six hours (or more for weak leavens), so be patient and observe the dough regularly.

When the dough has risen by one-third, tip it out of the container onto your benchtop, using a spatula to remove every bit of dough.

If you're making your first loaf, you can jump ahead now to step 9, the final shaping of the dough.

To learn more about bulk fermentation, see page 130.

7 Divide the dough

When you're working with larger quantities of dough and making more than one loaf, it's at this point that you'll divide the dough into smaller portions.

For your first bake, you're making only one loaf, so you don't need to divide the dough. You can go straight to step 9.

To learn more about dividing the dough, see page 136.

Preshape the dough

When you reach this step, if you're making a free-form loaf – that is, a loaf baked without a tin or any other structural support – you will preshape the dough once if it has great gluten strength or twice if the preshape isn't holding. Allow the dough to rest on the benchtop for 15 minutes after each shaping.

For your first loaf, you're baking the loaf in a tin, so you don't need to preshape it. You can go straight to step 9.

To learn more about preshaping, see page 138.

9 Final shape the dough

The final shaping of the dough creates a shape to suit how it will be baked (tin or free-form) and surface tension. For your first loaf, follow the final-shaping instructions for a tin loaf on page 142.

10 Transfer the dough

Lightly grease the interior of your bread tin, using olive oil or any other mildly flavoured vegetable oil.

Carefully scoop up the dough with both hands and place it gently into the tin, with the seam facing down.

Take a moment to note the dough's height in relation to the top of the tin. It's a good idea to take two photos of the dough – one from the side and one from above – to help you remember the height of the dough when it was first put in the tin.

To learn more about transferring the dough, see page 148.

11 Proof the dough

This is the second and final ferment prior to baking, during which you want the dough to rise almost to its fullest possible height: 90% of its maximum rise. (The final part of the rise happens during baking and is called 'oven spring'.)

For more information about oven spring, see page 164.

To make sure you can fit this first bake into one day, I'm going to ask you to speed up this second ferment by using the oven. It's important to realise that this isn't how you always have to do it: you have several proofing options.

For other proofing options, see page 154.

Leaving the oven switched *off*, place a large tray or dish capable of holding liquid on the oven floor. Bring the kettle to the boil, then carefully pour boiling water into the tray, until it is three-quarters full.

Put the tin containing the dough onto the top shelf of the oven. Close the oven door and allow the dough to proof in the steamy oven for one hour.

Check on the dough after the hour by removing it from the oven and taking more photos. Observe the height differences between the first and latest photos of the dough.

Now, with a clean finger, poke the dough confidently, then immediately take your hand away. The dough should spring back quickly to show it is still fermenting. Put the dough back in the oven and close the oven door. Leave it for 15 minutes, then remove the dough from the oven and poke it again. It should once again spring back quickly.

This time, cover the dough with a plastic bag or large upturned bowl, then leave it on the benchtop.

Place an oven rack as high as possible in the oven while leaving enough room for the dough in its tin plus an extra 10 cm (4 in) for the final rise (oven spring).

Top up the tray on the oven floor with more boiling water from the kettle.

Close the oven door and switch the oven on to 250°C (475°F) fan-forced.

By this point, the dough has proofed for just over 1 hour and 15 minutes. It will need to proof for longer before you see a considerable increase in its height. Keep poking it at regular intervals, until it no longer springs back quickly.

The moment the dough has increased considerably, looks lofty and billowy, and springs back slowly, it's time to bake.

To learn more about proofing the dough, see page 154.

12 Bake the bread

Check the oven temperature. When it reaches 250°C (475°F), put the tin containing the dough into the oven on the high shelf. It should take between 20 and 35 minutes for the bread to bake.

After 20 minutes, open the oven door and check on the loaf. Look at its colour, then turn it around and look at the other side. If it is browning more on one side than the other, rotating the tin will result in a more even bake. If it's browning too quickly on top, place it on a lower shelf.

If the top of the bread is evenly golden brown, using an oven glove, slide the oven shelf holding the loaf towards you until you can safely use a knuckle to knock on the top of the loaf. Does it sound hollow? If so, the bread is ready.

Alternatively, insert a food thermometer into the bread. If its internal temperature has reached 95°C (203°F) or above, the bread is ready.

If the bread isn't ready, return it to the oven, close the oven door and wait a few more minutes, then check it again. It shouldn't need longer than 40 minutes.

To learn more about baking the bread, see page 162.

Cool the bread

When the bread is ready, put a cooling rack on the benchtop. The rack should have legs so that its base sits above the benchtop, allowing air to pass underneath.

Turn off the oven and, using oven gloves, remove the tin containing the bread. Straightaway (and while still wearing the oven gloves), holding the tin over the cooling rack, slowly tip the tin and allow the bread to slip out. Place the bread bottom-side down on the rack. If you don't put the bread on the rack immediately, it will sweat and go moist, soft and terrible.

Allow the loaf to fully cool down before slicing it, to ensure the bread's crumb (its internal texture) isn't squashed.

When the loaf is completely cool, if you're not going to eat it straightaway, store it in an airtight container. Enjoy, beautiful humans.

To learn more about letting the bread cool, see page 166.

PART 2

The Baker's Percentage

I love the Baker's Percentage. It gives me flexibility with my baking, allowing me to fit baking in with my other passions. And it gives me the freedom to create my own recipes for different types of breads as well as the option to scale up from one to a dozen loaves and back down again, depending on what I need.

It's such a liberating way to make bread, at times spontaneously and on the fly, and at other times – like when I'm making an enriched dough, such as panettone – with careful precision. It's for this reason I was so motivated to write this book. Once you understand it, you too will be able to bake with abandon.

CHAPTER 5

Baker's Percentage basics

In the Baker's Percentage, the total weight of the flour is always stated as 100%. Think in weights, not volumes.

What is the Baker's Percentage?

The Baker's Percentage is a very simple calculating system that allows bakers to create bread recipes, to scale their recipes up and down, and to adjust recipes to suit their schedules, flavour preferences and available ingredients.

The system uses the *total weight of the flour* in a recipe as the basis for all the other ingredients' individual weights. The total weight of the flour is always, *always* stated as 100%. This means the total percentage of all ingredients, including the flour, is always *more than* 100%.

If you're using a total of 650 g (23 oz) of flour, that weight is expressed as 100% in the Baker's Percentage formula. If you're using a total of 1.5 kg (53 oz) of flour, that weight is *also* expressed as 100% in the formula.

The weight of every other ingredient is expressed as a percentage relative to the flour's 100%. As there are only three other ingredients in sourdough bread (water, leaven, salt), it doesn't take long to work out the weights we need.

As I said at the start of the book, for home bakers, the most important thing to know about the Baker's Percentage is that the *formula isn't fixed*.

Baker's Percentage calculations

There are some basic, easy-to-use calculations with the Baker's Percentage system, which I've outlined in the sections below. They will enable you to:

- convert Baker's Percentage formulas to ingredients weights, so you can measure out your ingredients accurately
- convert ingredients weights to Baker's Percentage formulas, to help you analyse and adapt other people's recipes
- scale recipes up or down, meaning you can make larger or smaller batches while keeping the ingredients proportions the same
- add extra ingredients like seeds, nuts and fruits without compromising the size of your dough.

It's vital to understand that all ingredients – including water – are measured by their *weight* when we're converting from percentages. We are never going to be measuring volumes. You need to think in grams and kilograms, not millilitres and litres, or in pounds and ounces, not cups and fluid ounces.

When you've got the hang of the calculations, in the following chapters I'll show you how to use them to adjust flavour, fermentation speed and even the types of sourdough breads you make.

CONVERT BAKER'S PERCENTAGE FORMULAS TO INGREDIENTS WEIGHTS

You'll need this calculation whenever you use a Baker's Percentage formula that you've created yourself or that your local baker has given you: you'll want to convert the percentages to weights in order to make the bread.

When you know your total flour weight, use the Baker's Percentage formula to calculate the weight of each of the other ingredients in turn, using this equation:

$$\frac{\text{(ingredient percentage)}}{\text{100 (flour percentage)}} \times \text{(total flour weight)} = \text{(total ingredient weight)}$$

For example, let's say you're making a single loaf of bread with a total of 400 g (14 oz) flour and a formula of 100% flour (as always), 65% water, 20% leaven and 2% salt. You would calculate the weights of the other ingredients as shown below. (The equations here use metric weights for clarity; to calculate the imperial weights, just change the total flour weight figure from 400 g to 14 oz.)

WATER

$$\frac{\text{65 (water percentage)}}{\text{100 (flour percentage)}} \times \text{400 (total flour weight)} = \text{260 (total water weight)}$$

LEAVEN

$$\frac{\text{20 (leaven percentage)}}{\text{100 (flour percentage)}} \times \text{400 (total flour weight)} = \text{80 (total leaven weight)}$$

SALT

$$\frac{\text{2 (salt percentage)}}{\text{100 (flour percentage)}} \times \text{400 (total flour weight)} = \text{8 (total salt weight)}$$

You end up with the following amounts:

INGREDIENTS	BAKER'S PERCENTAGE (%)	WEIGHT (G / OZ)
Flour	100	400 / 14
Water	65	260 / 9.17
Leaven	20	80 / 2.82
Salt	2	8 / 0.28

CONVERT INGREDIENTS WEIGHTS TO BAKER'S PERCENTAGE FORMULAS

Below is the equation to turn to when you have ingredients amounts in weights and you want to work out the Baker's Percentage formula:

$$\frac{\text{(total ingredient weight)}}{\text{(total flour weight)}} \times 100 \text{ (flour percentage)} = \text{(ingredient percentage)}$$

We'll use the same example as in the opposite section, except we're starting with ingredients weights: a single loaf of bread made with 400 g flour, 260 g water, 80 g leaven and 8 g salt. As always, we know the total weight of the flour will be expressed as 100%. The calculations for the percentages of the other ingredients look like this:

WATER

$$\frac{260 \text{ (total water weight)}}{400 \text{ (total flour weight)}} \times 100 \text{ (flour percentage)} = 65 \text{ (water percentage)}$$

LEAVEN

$$\frac{80 \text{ (total leaven weight)}}{400 \text{ (total flour weight)}} \times 100 \text{ (flour percentage)} = 20 \text{ (leaven percentage)}$$

SALT

$$\frac{8 \text{ (total water weight)}}{400 \text{ (total flour weight)}} \times 100 \text{ (flour percentage)} = 2 \text{ (salt percentage)}$$

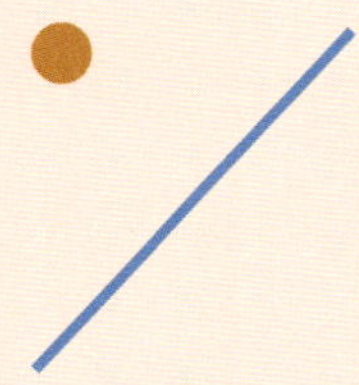

FLOUR COMBINATIONS

If you want to try mixing different types of flours in a loaf, the Baker's Percentage makes this easy to do, as all the other ingredients are calculated as a percentage of the *total* flour weight. For example, I could mix together:

200 g (7 oz) white flour
400 g (14 oz) wholegrain spelt flour
100 g (3.5 oz) wholegrain rye flour

The total flour weight is 700 g (24.7 oz), expressed as 100%. The other ingredients are calculated against this total.

(In this example, I've included a large proportion of wholegrain flour, in the form of the rye and spelt flours. Wholegrain flours absorb a lot of water, so to ensure the dough is adequately moist, I'll have to increase my water (hydration) percentage to something like 75–80%.)

For more information about hydration percentages, see Chapter 6.

SCALE RECIPES UP AND DOWN

What if you want to make more or less of the same bread? To get the same consistency, texture and crumb, you need to keep the ingredients at the same amounts relative to each other, while increasing or decreasing their actual weights. The Baker's Percentage system makes doing this a breeze.

We're using the same example again: 400 g flour and a formula of 100% flour, 65% water, 20% leaven and 2% salt.

Let's say we want to make three loaves instead of one. The original formula called for 400 g flour. To make three times that amount, we simply need to multiply the original flour weight by three:

400 (original total flour weight) × 3 = 1200 (new total flour weight)

So, the total flour weight is now 1200 g (42 oz). To find the new weight of every other ingredient, we use the 'convert Baker's Percentage formulas to ingredients weights' equation given on page 56.

The final results will be:

WATER

$$\frac{65 \text{ (water percentage)}}{100 \text{ (flour percentage)}} \times 1200 \text{ (total flour weight)} = 780 \text{ (total water weight)}$$

LEAVEN

$$\frac{20 \text{ (leaven percentage)}}{100 \text{ (flour percentage)}} \times 1200 \text{ (total flour weight)} = 240 \text{ (total leaven weight)}$$

SALT

$$\frac{2 \text{ (salt percentage)}}{100 \text{ (flour percentage)}} \times 1200 \text{ (total flour weight)} = 24 \text{ (total salt weight)}$$

To scale a recipe down, instead of *multiplying* the original weight of the flour by a factor of, say, two or three, we *divide* the original flour weight by the required amount to find the new total flour weight. Then, to calculate the weights of the other ingredients, use the same method as above for converting percentages to weights.

INGREDIENTS	BAKER'S PERCENTAGE (%)	WEIGHT (G / OZ)
Flour	100	1200 / 42
Water	65	780 / 27.5
Leaven	20	240 / 8.46
Salt	2	24 / 0.84

The maths might seem daunting at first, but believe me: it's easy. I am very bad at maths, but this is simple and makes bread baking extremely rewarding.

ADD EXTRA INGREDIENTS

When it comes to adding dried fruit, nuts, spices or other ingredients to a sourdough loaf, you can be playful with the amounts you use. You can initially use a handful of this and a pinch of that, and later, with the next loaf, try a little more or a little less, with no need to weigh out these extra ingredients.

Should you decide that you want to perfect and replicate a particular bread by calculating the proportion of that handful or that pinch, the Baker's Percentage is perfect for this. Simply translate the weights of the extra ingredients into percentages, using the calculation on page 57.

For example, if a handful of nuts weighed 50 g (1.76 oz) and a pinch of spice weighed 1 g (0.03 oz), and if your total flour weight was 600 g (21 oz), that would mean a Baker's Percentage of 8.3% for the nuts and 0.16% for the spice. When you wanted to make more than one loaf or to change the weight of the dough, you would just use these percentages.

If you incorporate a large amount of extra ingredients, your final dough will become bigger, and you will therefore need to use a bigger tin or proofing basket (banneton) to ensure the dough has the room it needs for the final proof. Alternatively, you can reduce the size of the dough by reducing the amount of the four key ingredients, to compensate for the extra ingredients. This is where the Baker's Percentage is extremely useful, as it allows you to easily work out how to reduce the flour, leaven, water and salt while retaining the same proportions.

The Baker's Percentage range

As we've seen, when you use the Baker's Percentage, the total weight of the flour is stated as 100%, and the weight of every other ingredient is expressed as a percentage relative to the total flour weight.

For sourdough breads, the total salt weight in relation to the total flour weight is fairly static, unless you have a health condition that requires you to alter it. Nearly all breads have a salt percentage of 2%.

But the other two main ingredients, the water (hydration) and the leaven, have a *range* of possible percentages. It's by adjusting these percentages in relation to the flour that you can change the structural strength of your dough (besides kneading), the level of gelatinisation (glistening) achieved in the bread crumb, the types of breads you make, the speed at which the dough ferments and the amount of sourness you incorporate into that dough (when working with a sour leaven).

For sourdough bread, with flour always at 100% and salt usually at 2%, the Baker's Percentage ranges for the other two ingredients, and the main factors that can influence them, are as follows:

INGREDIENTS	RANGE (%)	INFLUENCES
Water	60–100	Type of flour; type of bread
Leaven	5–40	Fermentation speed; acidity of leaven; type of bread

In the following two chapters, we'll discuss the Baker's Percentage ranges of water and leaven in more detail.

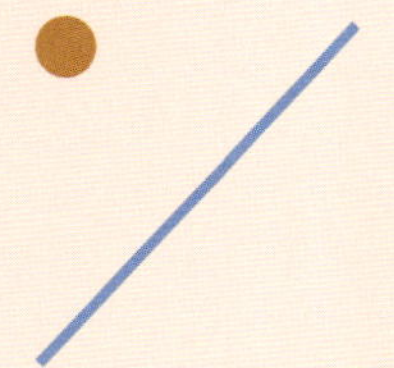

LEAVEN INGREDIENTS AND THE BAKER'S PERCENTAGE

We've been calculating Baker's Percentage formulas using the leaven as a separate ingredient. But of course, when you incorporate leaven into your dough, you're incorporating extra flour and water, the leaven's original ingredients.

Therefore, the actual flour and water weights are a little higher in comparison to the amount of salt in the formulas, and this means the actual percentages of the ingredients are slightly different from the percentages we've been calculating here.

But for day-to-day baking, you won't need to worry about this finer detail. Just use the basic version of the Baker's Percentage formula as shown in this chapter and use your observations and the feel of the dough to decide whether to adjust the formula. That's what I do.

CHAPTER 6

Hydration range

In sourdough bread, the Baker's Percentage hydration range is 60–100%. Higher hydrations speed up fermentation, and lower hydrations slow it down.

Hydration basics

Bread bakers refer to the percentage expressing the weight of water relative to the total weight of flour used in their recipes as the 'hydration' percentage. For example, a starter or a dough may be described as having 70% hydration or 80% hydration. I'll be using 'hydration' to refer to water content from this point.

In sourdough bread, the Baker's Percentage hydration range is 60–100%. Remember that this percentage is calculated against the total flour weight, which is always 100%. A dough with 100% hydration has the same total weight of water as its total weight of flour.

You can influence the structural strength of your dough (besides kneading), the gelatinisation of the bread crumb and the type of bread being made with the hydration percentage you use.

The hydration percentage is governed mainly by the protein (gluten) content of the flour (hard flour or soft flour) or by the amount of wholegrain flour used. Alternatively, it's determined by the type of bread being made; for example, pan de cristal and focaccia use very high hydrations combined with high-gluten flours. The table on page 64 summarises the basic information you need when considering your hydration percentage.

It's important to note that the structural strength of your dough is influenced not only by the amount of kneading you do, but also by its hydration. If a dough is too wet, it will not be able to hold its shape when a free-form loaf like a boule (round) or bâtard (oval) is made. A dough that is too dry, on the other hand, will not be able to stretch and rise effectively during fermentation and baking, nor will it give adequate starch gelatinisation.

Some bread bakers push their hydrations as high as they can (within the boundaries imposed by the flour), because of the gelatinisation that results. Others work with very high hydrations to produce specialty breads like focaccia and pan de cristal.

Some home bakers like to produce extremely wet doughs, because the process of making them has a reduced number of steps. These doughs are mixed in a bowl with a wooden spoon, allowed to bulk ferment, poured into a well-oiled tin for the proof and then baked. The resulting bread is usually flat topped but still delicious. The compromise in aesthetics means an easy recipe and regular home-baked bread.

When you come to understand how hydration percentages affect your bread's ability to hold its shape (structural strength), how flours differ in their capacity to absorb water (because of their gluten or wholegrain content), how very high hydrations create different breads and how hydration affects gelatinisation, you will be able to better modify bread-baking recipes or to create successful recipes of your own.

The table below gives you parameters to work with, but please note that they should be used as guides only.

<table>
<tr><th>HYDRATION (%*)</th><th>DOUGH CHARACTERISTICS</th><th>BREAD CHARACTERISTICS</th><th>BREAD TYPES</th></tr>
<tr><td>10–20**</td><td>· Very smooth, silky dough
· Excellent extensibility and stretch</td><td>Very soft, light, fluffy, sweet and fine crumb</td><td>· Breads made with all high-protein (13%+) white bread flour
· Low-fibre celebration breads
· Brioche, panettone</td></tr>
<tr><td>60–65</td><td>· Smooth dough
· Modest extensibility and stretch</td><td>· Open or closed crumb
· Moderate gelatinisation of bread crumb</td><td>· Standard loaf breads made with low-protein (8–10%) flours</td></tr>
<tr><td>70–75</td><td>· Smooth dough
· High extensibility and stretch</td><td>· Open or closed crumb
· Moderate gelatinisation of bread crumb</td><td>· Standard loaf breads made with all high-protein (12%+) white bread flour
· Very low-fibre breads</td></tr>
<tr><td rowspan="4">75–85</td><td colspan="3">WHOLEGRAIN</td></tr>
<tr><td>· Highly textured, sticky dough
· Minimal extensibility and stretch</td><td>· Closed crumb
· Heavy</td><td>Breads made with all wholegrain flours</td></tr>
<tr><td colspan="3">WHITE</td></tr>
<tr><td>· Very smooth, sticky dough
· High extensibility and stretch</td><td>· Medium to very open crumb
· Chewy bread</td><td>Breads made with very high gluten (13%+), all white flour</td></tr>
<tr><td>85–100</td><td>· Very smooth, extremely sticky dough
· Extremely extensible</td><td>· Open crumb
· Flat dough, not expected to hold a boule or bâtard shape</td><td>· Very high gluten (13%+), all white flour breads
· Ciabatta, focaccia, pan de cristal</td></tr>
</table>

* Approximate percentage expressing the weight of water relative to the total weight of flour.
** Milk only, with the remaining hydration coming from eggs, leaven, alcohol and butter.

SPECIALTY BREADS AND HYDRATION

The Italian word 'ciabatta' means 'slipper', as in house slippers. This name is used to describe a type of bread whose flatness and shape remind Italians of their comfy winter slippers. The Spanish, on the other hand, call a similar loaf 'pan de cristal', which means 'glass bread', due to the bread's thin crust and large, airy holes, which resemble crystal glass.

Both breads are produced from high-hydration doughs. Ciabatta typically has a hydration of around 85%, while pan de cristal's hydration can go as high as 100%.

The resulting doughs are tricky to handle, because they are loose, sticky and very extensible. But with the coil-fold kneading technique explained on page 123, they eventually build enough strength to hold a loose, flat shape. They have a very open crumb – particularly the Spanish version.

Unlike lower hydration doughs, which can be shaped any which way and will hold their shape, these doughs are not expected to hold a boule or bâtard form.

Flour and hydration

The protein (gluten) content of the flour you use has a huge influence on the amount of water the flour can absorb and, therefore, on the possible hydration percentage of your bread.

HIGH-PROTEIN FLOURS

The reason why most bread books ask you to purchase 'bread flour' or 'strong flour' is that it has a high protein (gluten) content (typically around 12–14%), and flours with higher amounts of gluten can absorb more water, meaning they can be used in high-hydration doughs. These flours are called 'strong' because their high gluten content allows them to stretch (rise) well during fermentation and baking and to be excellent at retaining their shape. This is desired by most bread bakers, because the resulting loaves burst high in the oven, creating those lovely 'ear' flaps on the top, with a glistening crumb that is open and airy, light and fluffy.

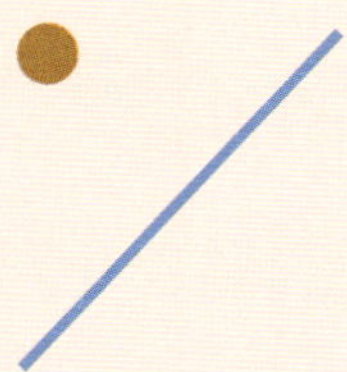

PROTEIN (GLUTEN) CONTENT BASICS

High-protein flours: **('hard' or 'strong' flours) are good at absorbing water. They are used to produce well-risen breads with ears that burst open and a crumb that is open, airy and glistening. Their protein content is typically around 12–14%.**

Low-protein flours: **('soft' or 'weak' flours) absorb less water. They are used for producing pastry, cakes and biscuits (cookies). Their protein content is typically around 8–10%.**

Medium-protein flours: **('plain' or 'all-purpose' flours) are designed for cooks working with a variety of recipes, from biscuits and cakes to breads, and who don't want to buy specialty flours for each one. These flours have moderate absorbency and aren't so capable of creating bread doughs that stretch easily or hold their shape. Their protein content is typically 11.7%.**

It's important to realise that within the high-protein category, each flour will have a different protein content. If you use a flour with a different protein content from the flour used by a recipe's author, the amount of water prescribed in the recipe may lead to your dough being either too dry or too wet. If, for example, you're using a flour that becomes too wet and loose after adding the water stipulated in a recipe, it simply means that the flour has a gluten content too low to let it absorb that much water. Don't despair. After your initial mix, simply add more flour and mix well again. Next time, just use a lower hydration.

Variations in bread flour protein contents are especially noticeable between different countries. For example, Australian bread flours usually have a protein content of around 12–12.3%, while Italy typically produces bread flours with a 13.5% protein content, and the United States' bread flours tend to have a 14.2% protein content. While these numerical differences might seem very small, they greatly influence the hydration capacity of your bread dough.

When you learn about the attractions of high-protein flours, it can be tempting to think that to get a loftier free-form loaf with a more open crumb, all you need to do is increase the strength of your flour. However, to achieve an open-crumb dough, all stages of the bread-making process need to be well understood and managed. Enjoy the process of learning about each core bread-baking step, as all the elements need to work together for you to achieve the results you desire.

FREE-FORM LOAVES

A stronger bread flour is particularly important if you want to make free-form loaves – that is, loaves not baked in a tin. The 'no-knead' recipes often used to create free-form loaves, if made with a lower-gluten flour, will produce a weak dough incapable of supporting its shape. The loaf subsequently won't burst open during baking, and it will be flatter than you might want. The bread remains delicious and nutritious, though, regardless of its shape.

WHOLEGRAIN FLOURS

Wholegrain – including wholemeal (whole-wheat) – flours, like strong bread flour, have a high protein content (around 12%). This means that they too can absorb plenty of water, so they are used with high hydration percentages (75–85%).

However, the high protein levels from these flours come from protein contained in their germ and bran, which isn't the type of protein that develops into gluten. In fact, the germ and bran have a negative impact on gluten and undermine its structure-building potential. To reduce this negative impact, some bakers autolyse or fermentolyse their wholegrain flours for an hour before adding the leaven, as the longer hydration time softens the sharp edges of the germ and bran.

The overall result, therefore, is flour with a high protein content but less gluten than white flour. The gluten in wholegrain flours is 'diluted' by the germ and bran content, creating heavier, denser loaves.

But the word 'wholemeal' is a reminder that only when we eat the whole meal do we get what is best for us: a high amount of fibre. And in the absence of adequate fibre, well, you know what happens.

LOW-PROTEIN FLOURS

If for any reason you're using a white flour with a very low gluten content (below 11%), you'll need to start mixing your dough with a low hydration percentage, say 60%, and increase the hydration from there if the flour can handle it. But if your flour can only take lower hydrations, look into sourcing a stronger bread flour.

Higher hydrations are possible with lower-protein flours if the bread is baked in a tin. This is because the tin will support the sides of the dough, no matter how wet it is.

If your flour is particularly low in gluten, you can try adding some gluten flour, which is also called 'vital wheat gluten'. **For information about gluten flour, see page 99.**

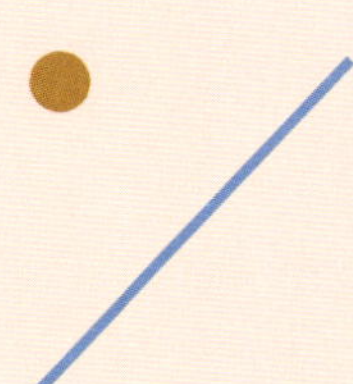

KNEADING AND DOUGH HYDRATION

The amount of kneading you do affects how well a dough absorbs water and the amount of water that evaporates during the knead. You may start with a dough that feels too wet, but after adequate kneading it will come together beautifully. Therefore, don't despair if your dough initially feels too sticky and wet.

High-hydration doughs need to be kneaded for longer than low-hydration doughs, because the high water content dilutes the concentration of gluten. And with very high hydrations, such as those used for pan de cristal and ciabatta, coil folds are used to deal with the fluid doughs.

Also, in wholegrain flour doughs, a higher hydration is necessary because the germ and bran in the whole grains are capable of absorbing high volumes of water. Wholegrain doughs will feel very sticky, but after considerable kneading most will start to become a smooth, cohesive mass. Wholegrain rye, however, will continue to feel very sticky all the way through the knead, regardless of kneading time.

Some Italian wholegrain flours perform very differently from other wholegrain flours when mixed with a very high hydration of 85–90%, in that after a long autolyse or fermentolyse combined with extensive kneading, the gluten development is extremely good, producing a remarkable windowpane.
For more information about kneading, see page 116.

Starter and leaven hydration

STARTER HYDRATION

For the starter recipe on page 32, which used wholemeal (whole-wheat) flour, you used a hydration percentage of 100% (remember that wholegrain flours absorb a lot of water). I wanted the fermentation to be clearly noticeable, and this level of hydration with a wholemeal flour produces a thick starter with large, visible bubbles. I chose this hydration percentage based on fermentation visibility, not fermentation speed.

However, I could have increased the hydration of the starter to be 170%, 180% or more. I could have produced a very loose, liquid-like starter consistency, resulting in a faster fermentation with smaller bubbles. A starter can be made to be very firm or very loose, and every recipe you come across will differ in terms of both the flour used to make the starter and the hydration percentage.

Had I asked you to use a white bread flour, however, a hydration of 150% would have been too high and would have resulted in a watery starter, making it hard for a beginner baker to discern fermentation. More importantly, it would have produced a leaven far too wet for a typical sourdough recipe.

LEAVEN HYDRATION

Leaven can also be made with varying levels of hydration: 100% hydration, 50% hydration, lower if you use the pinch-of-dough method and higher if you're using wholegrain flours.

For information about the pinch-of-dough method, see page 91.

Hydration can also be expressed as a ratio. For example, a hydration ratio of 1:1 means one part flour to one part water, or 100 g (3.5 oz) flour to 100 g (3.5 oz) water.

Hydration affects the leaven's fermentation speed. If all other factors, such as feeding schedules and room temperature, are kept the same, higher hydrations speed up fermentation, and lower hydrations slow it down. Understanding this means you can adjust your leaven hydration according to your bread-making schedule.

If, for example, you want to slow down leaven fermentation between bakes, you can choose a low to very low leaven hydration combined with fridge temperature ferment. If you need fermentation to happen in time for a bake later in the day, you can choose a higher hydration combined with a room temperature ferment to ensure the leaven is ready to use.

HYDRATION, TEMPERATURE, FEEDING AND LEAVEN SOURNESS

Both hydration and temperature can speed up or slow down fermentation, and a baker can use this knowledge to manage their leaven's sourness (acidity). Sourness is produced the moment fermentation begins and continues to be produced as fermentation progresses. The word 'progresses' is important here. A leaven will reach maximum fermentation (maximum height and carbon dioxide production) and then start to fall (progress), and acids (as well as some ethanol) will continue to form and build up.

A baker who wants their bread to never be sour can use one, or all, or a combination, of the following three options:

1. **Reduce the leaven's temperature by placing it in the fridge.**
2. **Reduce the leaven's hydration by making it very firm, using the smallest amount of water possible.**
3. **Adjust the frequency with which the leaven is fed.**

For information about feeding your leaven, see page 112.

Don't confuse placing the *leaven* in the fridge to slow down its fermentation with cold proofing or cold bulk fermenting the *dough* in the fridge.

In fact, here's something to ponder. The interest in creating sourdough with an open crumb and very low levels of sourness has led some bakers to feed their leavens twice a day every day at room temperature, followed by a fridge bulk fermentation or fridge proof to develop complex flavours.

A home baker needs to consider whether all this effort is worth it. Why not just work with a leaven that is slightly sour, slower at fermenting, but packed with the flavour you wanted in the first place? I recommend leaving fridge bulk fermentation and proofing to when you need to slow fermentation down for other reasons, like riding your bike to go and see live music or a friend.

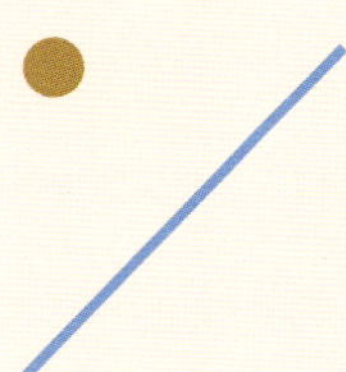

HYDRATION PERCENTAGES FOR FIRST-TIME BAKERS

While you're learning, I'd recommend a couple of options for testing your dough's (that is, your flour's) hydration percentage capacity. For both options, make sure your flour has a high protein (gluten) content of around 12%. Then, try one of the following:

- **Start with a hydration of around 68% and increase it with each loaf you make, for as long as the dough can absorb the water without a final free-form loaf flattening out.**
- **Start with a 68% hydration; make sure you mix the water, leaven, salt and flour very well; and allow the dough to rest for 30 minutes, to fermentolyse. This rest is the first rest that occurs in the core steps. After the 30-minute fermentolyse, add a little more water if the dough feels too stiff. (As a beginner, it's going to be difficult to know what 'too stiff' feels like, but you'll quickly get the hang of it once you've done a few bakes.) Then mix that water in extremely well, followed by a 15-minute rest before your first knead.**

A BAKING SCHEDULE FOR A FREE-FORM LOAF

Francesca works from home. She bakes a free-form loaf once a week using a flameproof casserole dish (Dutch oven). She uses white flour with 12.3% protein content and a mildly sour and weak leaven (150% hydration, wholegrain rye flour).

Francesca made a starter a month ago and matured it into a leaven. She keeps her leaven in the fridge and feeds it once a week during a bake.

She sometimes kneads by hand and sometimes uses her machine mixer with a dough hook. Today, she's using her hands. She uses the Baker's Percentage formula below to calculate the ingredients weights for a total flour weight of 550 g (19.4 oz).

- 450 g (15.9) white bread flour
- 100 g (3.5 oz) wholemeal (whole-wheat) flour
- 412.5 g (14.5 oz) water
- 110 g (3.88 oz) leaven
- 11 g (0.39 oz) salt

INGREDIENTS	BAKER'S PERCENTAGE (%)	WEIGHT (G / OZ)
Flour	100	550 / 19.4
Water	65	412.5 / 14.5
Leaven	20	110 / 3.88
Salt	2	11 / 0.39

1 **8 am – Prepare the leaven.** Francesca removes her leaven from the fridge to bring it to room temperature.

2 **9 am – Combine and mix the ingredients.** To a large bowl, Francesca adds, in this order, the water, leaven, salt and flours. She mixes them extremely well, until there are no patches of dry flour to be seen.

3 **9.20 am – Rest the dough.** Francesca covers the dough with a wet tea towel and leaves it for 30 minutes to fermentolyse.

4 **Feed the leaven.** While the dough is resting, she feeds her leaven with flour and cold water (150% hydration, wholegrain rye flour), then returns it to the fridge.

5 **9.50 am – Knead the dough.** Francesca does 60 stretch and folds, then covers the dough and rests it for 15 minutes.

For kneading instructions, see page 121.

10.10 am – Francesca does another 60 stretch and folds, then covers the dough and rests it for a further 15 minutes.

6 **10.30 am – Let the dough bulk ferment.** Francesca does a windowpane test. The dough looks good, stretches well and creates a transparent pane, but she knows she will need to develop the gluten a little more. She doesn't have time to knead during the bulk fermentation, as she will be using those hours to complete a university assignment instead. So, she'll develop the gluten a little more during preshaping.

For information about the windowpane test, see page 119.

Francesca greases the inside of a rectangular, transparent plastic food container, then removes the dough from the bowl and places it in the container. She lightly wets her fingers and pushes the dough down firmly so that there are no gaps between the container and the dough and so that the dough height is level. Then she seals the lid on the container. She marks the level of the top of the dough with a piece of masking tape on the outside of the container.

Francesca is aware that her home is cool, sitting at around 19°C (65°F), and that this will slow down the bulk fermentation. She chooses to do the bulk fermentation at room temperature, so she can have an uninterrupted block of time to complete her studies. She sets her timer for four hours.

2.30 pm – Francesca checks on the bulk fermentation and can see it needs a little more time, as the dough hasn't risen by one-third. She gives it another hour.

7 **3.30 pm – Preshape and bench rest the dough.** The dough is now well fermented, with a clear one-third rise. Francesca tips the dough onto her benchtop. She doesn't need to divide it, as she's only making one loaf. She'll go straight into preshaping.

She drags the dough across the benchtop while rotating it and tucking its edges underneath it. With this motion she makes the dough rounder, smaller and tighter.

She leaves the dough to rest, covered by her dough-making bowl, for 15 minutes.

For preshaping instructions, see page 138.

3.50 pm – On her return, Francesca sees that the dough has loosened considerably and therefore takes the opportunity to use some kneading techniques to further develop the dough's strength, by doing a lamination fold followed by two coil folds.

She lets the dough rest, covered, for a further 15 minutes.

For lamination and coil fold instructions, see pages 123–24.

8 4.15 pm – Final shape the dough. Francesca returns and is excited to see the dough has held its shape far better this time. She knows that the final shape will be enough to create a well-supported dough.

She dusts the dough surface lightly with flour, then flips the dough so that the floured side is on the benchtop.

She stretches the dough out a little on all sides to create a rectangle, then folds the right side of the dough into the centre and folds the left side on top of the previous fold.

She grabs the end closest to her, stretches it out, and then folds it halfway across the first two folds. Finally, she stretches the end furthest from her and brings it across towards her, to cover all the other folds.

She rolls the dough towards her, so the seams are on the bottom of the dough.

Now she uses a drag, rotate and tuck motion to tension the dough. She has created a fantastic boule shape.

She gently spreads semolina flour over its entire upper surface, making a fine film. Her proofing basket is new and will stick to the dough if she doesn't dust it generously.

9 4.20 pm – Transfer the dough to the tin or proofing basket. Francesca lifts her dough off the benchtop and tips it gently to land seam side up in the basket. She does one more dusting of semolina flour, around the top of the dough, so that as it rises, the semolina will stop it sticking to the basket.

10 4.30 pm – Proof the dough. She wants the proof to happen quickly, so she can get an early night. Leaving the oven switched off, she puts a tray on the oven floor and pours boiling water into it. Then she places the basket holding the dough on the top rack in the oven and closes the oven door.

5.30 pm – After an hour, Francesca checks on the dough and does a poke test. The dough springs straight back, showing it isn't yet properly proofed. But it's time to turn the oven on, so she removes the dough from the oven and puts it on the benchtop, covered with a large bowl, to finish proofing at room temperature.

For information about the poke test, see page 156.

She removes the tray from the oven floor, places her flameproof casserole dish (Dutch oven) inside the oven, and switches the oven on at 250°C (475°F). The oven will need to preheat for one hour.

6.00 pm – Francesca checks on the dough again and does another poke test. The dough springs back slowly: it's ready for baking. But the oven needs to preheat for another 30 minutes, so Francesca places the basket holding the dough in a plastic bag and puts it in the fridge, to slow down fermentation.

6.25 pm – Francesca removes her dough from the fridge. She puts a piece of baking paper across the top of the dough basket and sits a round plate upside down over it, then flips the plate and basket to tip the dough onto the paper and plate. Leaving the basket covering the dough, she puts her oven gloves on and removes the flameproof casserole dish from the oven, putting it on the benchtop and setting the lid to one side.

11 6.30 pm – Bake the bread. Francesca takes the proofing basket off the plate and using a scoring lame makes four sharply angled cuts across the top of the dough.

Then, with a hand on either side of the dough, she takes hold of each edge of the baking paper, lifts the dough onto the paper, then lowers it – still on the paper – into the flameproof casserole dish. She puts her oven gloves back on, replaces the lid on the dish and puts it in the oven.

She sets her timer for 20 minutes, then sits down on her couch, full of excitement and anticipation.

6.50 pm – Twenty minutes have passed, so with oven gloves back on, Francesca opens the oven door, removes the heavy casserole dish lid and places it on her sink's metal draining board to cool. She leaves her gloves on top of the lid to remind her that it's super-hot and sets the timer for a further ten minutes.

7.00 pm – The boule is looking golden brown and gorgeous. Francesca pulls on the oven gloves and removes the dish holding the boule from the oven.

With her food thermometer, she stabs the middle of the loaf. The internal temperature has reached 95°C (203°F). She lifts the boule from the skillet and places it on a cooling rack on the benchtop.

12 Let the bread cool. Francesca lets the boule cool almost fully before cutting a few slices, which she smothers in butter. Happiness.

CHAPTER 7

Leaven range

There are multiple ways to feed and manage a leaven.

Leaven basics

In sourdough bread, the Baker's Percentage range for leaven is 5–40%. A quick reminder: this percentage is calculated against the total flour weight, which is always 100%. A dough with 20% leaven has a total weight that is 20% of the total weight of the flour.

You can influence the speed at which your doughs ferment, the flavour (sourness) of your breads and the types of breads you produce, depending on what leaven percentage you use. The below is a guide for how to approach leaven percentages when creating a bread recipe. Use it as a starting point from which to further develop your understanding of leaven use and play with percentages of your own.

LEAVEN (%*)	WHEN TO USE	FERMENTATION SPEED	BREAD SOURNESS	BREAD TYPES
5–10	• With very sour, weak leaven when you want to reduce the bread's sourness • Or with strong, not sour leaven when you want to greatly reduce the dough's fermentation speed	Slow**	Low	Sandwich loaf
15–20	• For moderate sourness with medium-strength leaven • Or for no sourness with strong leaven	Moderate to fast	Moderate to none	• Sandwich loaf • Focaccia • Pan de cristal
30	• For moderate sourness with medium-strength leaven • Or for no sourness with strong leaven	Moderate to fast	Moderate to none	Heavy fruit and nut breads
30–40	For no sourness with strong leaven	Fast	None	• Enriched breads • Panettone • Brioche

* Approximate percentage expressing the weight of leaven relative to the total weight of flour.
** For example, overnight bulk ferment at a room temperature of 19–22°C (65–70°F) or long day bulk ferment. This might be used when many loaves of bread are being made or to allow a baker to fit in other activities.

When to adjust the leaven percentage

LOW LEAVEN

Lower leaven percentages (5–10%) lead to slower fermentation. Many bakeries work with lower leaven percentages to allow them to keep up with preparing dozens of different doughs. For home bakers, knowing that you can make your dough ferment slowly is extremely helpful when you want to stretch out the bulk fermentation during the day to allow other activities to fit in.

Alternatively, if you can't fit in the bulk fermentation during the day, it allows you to do an overnight ferment, leaving the final steps to the following day. In other words, during the evening of one day, you can mix all the ingredients, allow the dough to rest, knead it, then leave it at room temperature to bulk ferment overnight, and in the morning, divide, shape, proof and bake. On very warm nights (35°C / 95°F and above), you can either decrease the amount of leaven you use in your recipe even further (say, to 2%) or complete the bulk fermentation in the fridge.

This type of flexibility is what will keep you baking for many years. There will be times when there is simply no room in the fridge to slow down fermentation, and that's when it is extremely helpful to know you can use a very low leaven percentage in your recipe instead. Lower leaven percentages also result in reduced leaven flavour in your bread. For example, if you have a very acidic, weak leaven and you don't have the time or the energy to discard and feed it multiple times to make it strong prior to using it, you can either use less of it and wait longer for bulk fermentation and proofing to occur or use less of it and work with warm ingredients (including warm water and ensuring the leaven is brought to room temperature) and a warm room (25–27°C / 75–80°F) to add a bit of speed to the fermentation.

For information about making a strong leaven, see page 85.

MODERATE LEAVEN

Leaven percentages in the middle of the range (15–20%) are some of the most used: many sourdough bread recipe books will have you using 20% leaven in your doughs. This amount of leaven is ideal when the leaven isn't too acidic.

HIGH LEAVEN

High leaven percentages (30–40%) are used to make some enriched breads, such as brioche or panettone, the Italian Christmas bread, as well as a range of breads that contain high volumes of fruit or nuts, or a combination of both. When using such a high percentage of leaven, though, it's important to use only strong leaven. Some bakers find the addition of a booster leaven to be helpful with these doughs, and some add dried yeast to an enriched sourdough bread.

For information about making a booster leaven, see page 86.

SPECIALTY BREADS AND LEAVEN

Panettone is an Italian celebration bread eaten at Christmas. The word 'panettone' means 'large bread'. It uses an enriched dough made heavy by the inclusion of lots of eggs, butter, milk, and dried fruit soaked in alcohol.

The weight of these additional ingredients combined with the introduction of alcohol and lactose, which slow down bacterial and yeast activity, means some bakers use a higher amount of leaven to support dough fermentation. A booster leaven is also sometimes used to further supercharge bacterial and yeast activity. The resulting bread is extremely fragrant with a light crumb.
For information about making a booster leaven, see page 86.

PART 3

Core steps in depth

In Chapter 4, I introduced you to the 13 core bread-baking steps all bakers follow to make bread. These core steps are essential and form the backbone of the bread-making process.

In Part 3, I'm going to give you more information about each of the core steps. The details within each step will allow you to make sense of differences in bread-baking approaches. For example, each baker has their own way to manage leaven and their own preferred kneading and shaping methods.

But remember that in order to reach the end point, regardless of which individual pathways they follow, all bakers need to pass the same key milestones: well-developed gluten, proper bulk fermentation, adequate proofing and so on.

So don't let differences confuse you. Knowing what options you have will help you to choose pathways that work for you and to make bread baking possible in the long term.

STEP 1

Prepare a leaven

In this step

For more information

Making your own starter and maturing it into a leaven is a fantastic way to learn more about fermentation, which is what sourdough baking is all about. The process involves daily observations to see if fermentation has started, if it's proceeding (increasing in height with lots of gas bubbles), if it has reached maximum carbon dioxide production (maximum height) and if it's slowing down (decreasing in height) or has come to a halt.

This is exactly the same process that occurs in your bread dough, giving you a clear idea of what to expect when you make your first loaf. Leaven is used in bread dough to make the dough rise.

Types of flours

You can use any flour you like to make a starter – spelt, emmer, white, rye, wheat – the process is the same. The fragrance and the size of the bubbles will be different, though. Wholegrain flours tend to produce big bubbles, especially if they're freshly milled.

You don't need to use the same type of flour for your starter and your leaven; you can continually change which flour you use. For example, you might make a starter using rye flour, and then, once it has matured into leaven, you could start feeding it only white flour, or spelt, or emmer, or wholegrain, or half-white half-rye. Any combination of flours will work.

Even when it isn't at its peak, leaven will cause bread dough to rise.

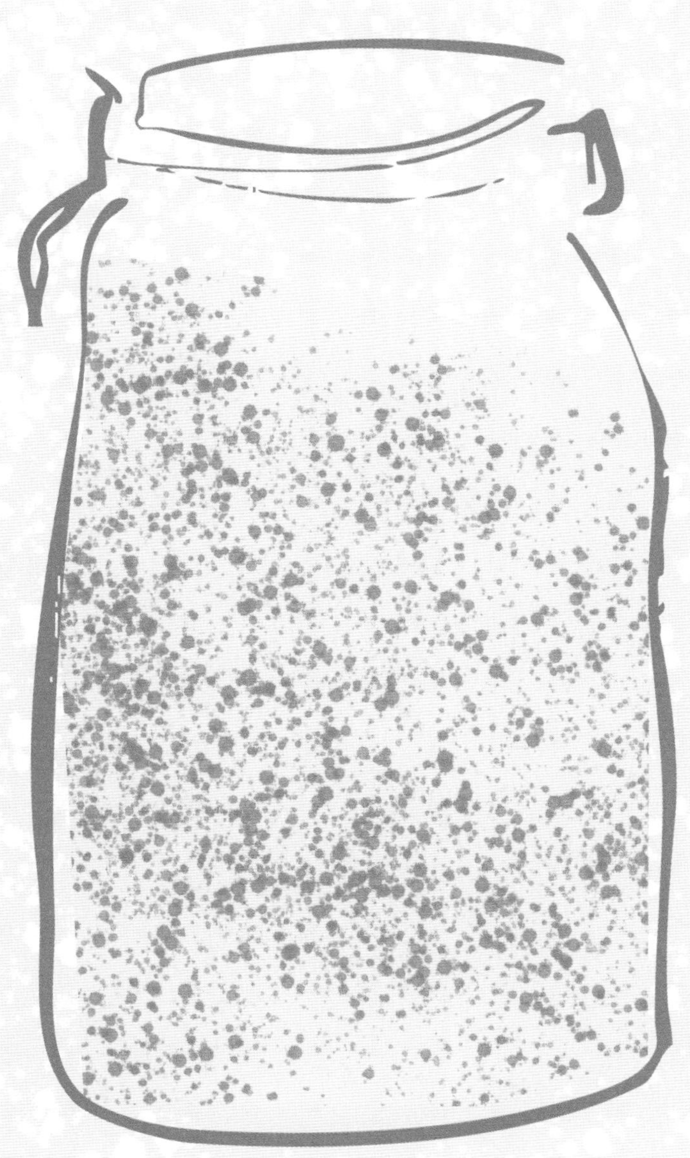

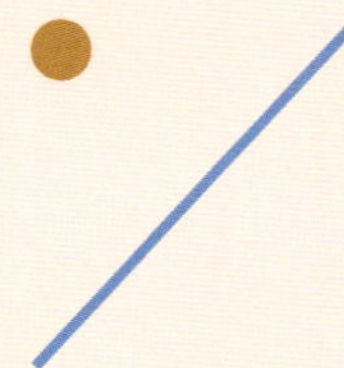

ETHANOL BUILD-UP IN A STARTER OR LEAVEN

If you notice a dark liquid on the top of your starter or leaven, please don't worry. That liquid is a build-up of ethanol, and it's telling you that you need to feed your starter or leaven more frequently or slow down its fermentation.

To solve a build-up of ethanol, tip out all but one teaspoon of starter or leaven, then add to that teaspoon fresh flour and water – enough to bring the weight up to what's needed for your next bake – to create a thick, pancake-like batter.

Allow it to ferment at room temperature, then either feed it more frequently or slow down its fermentation – by reducing its hydration (firm it up by using less water) or using the pinch-of-dough method, and by keeping it in the fridge.

For information about the pinch-of-dough method, see page 91.

Leaven strength

Leaven's strength is determined by the speed at which it ferments and doubles in volume. It is at its strongest when managed for strength and at its weakest when not managed for strength. A leaven becomes weak (slow to ferment), when acids (and ethanol), the by-products of fermentation, are allowed to build up, causing gluten degradation.

There are various ways of managing leaven for strength, all of which have validity and give the home baker the flexibility needed to continue baking. But it's important to know that as a home baker you can use a strong, medium-strength or weak leaven: you have that choice. You can make excellent tin loaves or closed-crumb free-form loaves with leaven at any strength, but you can only make open-crumb free-form loaves from leaven that is very strong.

As you don't need to fit in with a bakery schedule or with any clients' taste buds, you can choose to make bread that is very sour, or a little bit sour, or not sour at all. You can choose to use a leaven that is weak (and therefore sour) and use less of it for a mild-flavoured bread or nearly all of it for a strong-flavoured bread.

You can choose to manage leaven so that it is always strong and used at its peak performance, when it has reached maximum fermentation, or you can choose to manage leaven so that it is always of medium strength or weak. The leaven management pathway you choose is completely up to you, and the knowledge that you will gain from this section of the book will allow you to make an informed and sustained choice.

STRONG LEAVEN (VERY FAST FERMENTATION)

Qualities

- Strong leaven can ferment and double in volume within four hours of being fed.
- It can bulk ferment bread dough in four hours.
- It contains very small amounts of lactic and acetic acids, meaning there will be little or no sourness to the bread.
- It is a thick or thin, pancake-like batter, with an 80–140% hydration, or higher if only wholemeal (whole-wheat) or wholegrain rye flour is used to make it.
- Its gluten remains strong and has good structure.

Uses

- It is used when a very fast fermentation is needed.
- Strong leaven is used to make sourdough loaves with an open crumb and no sourness – for example, soup loaves, panettone and brioche.

How much to use in a bake

- The typical amount of strong leaven used for everyday baking is 20% (expressed as a Baker's Percentage).
- You can use anywhere from 5% to 40% strong leaven.
- You may need even less than 5% in hot periods when you do an overnight bulk ferment or proof at room temperature.

Care requirements

- Never store strong leaven in the fridge.
- Do twice-daily discards and feeds to to keep it strong, especially leading up to a bake.

BOOSTER LEAVEN

Some bakers use a booster leaven to further supercharge a strong leaven, to aid the development of an open crumb. On the morning of a bake, they make a new leaven – the booster – and mix it into an existing strong leaven that has had its twice-daily discards and feeds and therefore was fed the previous evening.

To make a booster, follow these instructions:

1. Take 1 tablespoon of the strong leaven and place in a clean jar.
2. Add to it 1 tablespoon of high-protein white flour and 1 tablespoon of water at 35°C (95°F). Mix very well.
3. Leave the jar containing the booster in a warm place (25–27°C / 75–80°F) for two hours.
4. After two hours take 1 teaspoon of the booster and drop it into a glass of water. If it clearly floats, it's ready. If it doesn't float, wait a little longer and then try another float test.
5. Once a teaspoon of booster floats, add the rest of the booster to your existing leaven, mix well, and use the combination to make your bread.

This kind of leaven management makes a lot of work for a home baker and may be something you use for special occasions rather than for week-to-week baking. But give it a try, to see how it affects your bread.

MEDIUM-STRENGTH LEAVEN (FAST FERMENTATION)

Qualities

- Medium-strength leaven takes five or more hours to ferment and double in volume.
- It can bulk ferment bread dough in five to six hours.
- It is mildly sour and will introduce a mild sourness to your bread.
- It is a thick or thin, pancake-like batter.
- It has some gluten degradation.

Uses

- This leaven can be used for any type of bread that does not require a very open crumb or a light, super-soft crumb, such as that needed for a panettone.
- It is suitable for breads that don't need a very fast fermentation.

How much to use in a bake

- You can use anywhere from 5% to 30% medium-strength leaven (expressed as a Baker's Percentage).

Care requirements

- Feed once a week on the day of a bake. No discard is produced, and only the leaven used in the bread recipe is removed before a feed.
- Keep it in the fridge between weekly bakes.

WEAK LEAVEN (SLOWER FERMENTATION)

Qualities

- Weak leaven can ferment and double in volume in seven or more hours.
- It can bulk ferment bread dough in eight or more hours.
- It contains a high volume of lactic and acetic acids, meaning there will be considerable sourness to the bread.
- It is a thick or thin, pancake-like batter.
- It has high gluten degradation.

Uses

- Weak leaven is best used in bread baked in a tin.
- It isn't suitable for open-crumb free-form loaves or enriched doughs.

How much to use in a bake

- You can use anywhere from 5% to 20% weak leaven (expressed as a Baker's Percentage).

Care requirements

- Keep this leaven in the fridge between infrequent bakes.
- Feed it when you do a bake.

SMELLY OLD LEAVEN?

What if you have weak leaven that looks poorly and smells like blue-vein cheese? I very much need you to know that I have made delicious bread from that kind of weak leaven, from leaven so weak that no book except this one would suggest using it. And yet this book exists because knowing that you *can* make delicious bread from weak, acidic leaven is completely liberating and will allow you to keep baking for decades.

If your leaven is in this kind of state and you don't have time to refresh it, or you're just too tired, but you're keen to have fresh bread for the next day, simply use a small amount – say, 2% of the total flour weight. The dough fermentation will be very slow – ten hours or more – allowing you to go to bed and then wake up to a completed bulk fermentation. By using a small leaven percentage, you'll have reduced both the amount of weakened gluten going into your dough and the amount of sourness in your bread.

A helpful thing to know is that, unless you intend to do so, you can't kill leaven. Many beginner bakers at some point think they've accidentally done just that. But to kill a leaven, you'd need to sterilise it. This would involve placing your leaven jar in a pot, covering it with water, bringing it to the boil and boiling it for ten minutes (at sea level, if you want the fine details). The yeast and bacteria in your leaven are *not easily killed.*

Having said that, if you ever see moulds of any colour on the surface of your leaven, throw it away or tip it into the garden, then make or acquire a new one.

Leaven fermentation

PEAK FERMENTATION

The speed at which leaven will make a bread dough rise depends in part on its stage of fermentation. Peak fermentation, the highest point of the leaven's rise, is the stage at which it will make dough rise most rapidly.

The best way to test whether your leaven has reached peak fermentation is to place a rubber band around your leaven jar marking the height of the leaven just after a feed. Keep the leaven with you, so you can watch it. As it rises, move the rubber band with the rise. Eventually, you won't see a rise above the rubber band, but a fall. At the highest point marked by the rubber band, peak fermentation was reached.

However, even when it isn't at its peak, leaven will cause bread dough to rise. When I first started baking, I was led to believe that I could only produce a successful loaf of bread if my leaven was so full of carbon dioxide – at the top of its rise – that it would float perfectly on the surface of water. Leaven that sank or only half-floated, I was told, could not be used. But this isn't the case. Home bakers can use leaven even when it sinks to the bottom; it will take longer to make your dough rise, but it will still work.

FERMENTATION SPEED

Both slow- and fast-fermenting leavens produce great bread. So, if fermentation speed is not important to you, and if you're not aiming for a very open crumb, and if you bake no more than once a week, then you can simply bring your leaven to room temperature when you need it and feed it only on the day when you're making bread. I can't emphasise enough how many home bakers, including me, are doing this and are producing excellent bread.

Unlike this book, most sourdough resources will tell you to keep your leaven at room temperature and to feed it twice every day to achieve maximum leaven fermentation speed on the day of the bake, get rid of all acidity and create an open crumb. But please know that as a home baker you have lots of options for managing both leaven fermentation speed and leaven acidity without doing once- or twice-daily feeds. In fact, it's so exciting when you understand all the different ways that leaven can be managed.

Leaven fermentation speed is affected by temperature and hydration:

- Warm temperatures speed up fermentation, and cold temperatures slow it down.
- Higher hydrations speed up fermentation, and lower hydrations slow it down.

Many bakers try to either slow down or speed up leaven fermentation between bakes based on how often they bake. People baking every day want fast fermentation between bakes, while less frequent bakers want slow fermentation between bakes: if leaven is allowed to ferment quickly between bakes but then becomes very acidic, it will be weak on the day of the bake, leading to a slower dough fermentation, an overly sour bread and a crumb less open than might be desired.

Controlling leaven fermentation speed *between* bakes controls both the leaven's acidity and the speed at which it ferments *on the day of* the bake.

Managing sourness and fermentation speed between bakes

When flour ferments, lactic acid, acetic acid and ethanol are produced. They create the delicious, complex, sour flavours in sourdough bread. But if they aren't managed, they can create too much acid, and hence too much sourness.

There are some sourdough bakers who love sourness and some who don't, and some of their family members and friends may love their sourdough bread with all sorts of different flavour profiles. Some sourdough bakers even want zero acidity in their breads. All these bakers will manage their leavens accordingly. To reduce the sourness (acidity) in sourdough, you have two options: either speed up leaven fermentation or slow it down between bakes.

Speed it up: To speed up fermentation, you need to discard some of the leaven – half or three-quarters of it – and then replace the discarded portion with a fresh batch of flour and water. This needs to be done every day, and sometimes two or three times a day.

The leaven will start to double or triple in volume within four hours of feeding and will never develop sourness.

Slow it down: There are various methods to slow down leaven fermentation between bakes:

- Make just enough leaven for your recipe, with only smears of leaven left behind in the jar. This will slow down fermentation, because so little leaven has been left in the jar to kickstart the next ferment. Also, if the leaven was particularly acidic, this approach will reduce acidity in the next ferment, as you'll be adding lots of fresh flour and water. When you feed, create a thick, pancake-like batter and store the leaven in the fridge.
- Make a very thick leaven – as thick as possible while ensuring that the flour is completely wet. The thicker the leaven is (that is, the lower the amount of water used), the slower the fermentation is between bakes. As soon as the leaven has been fed, store it in the fridge.
- On baking day, pinch a piece of dough the size of a golf ball from the dough you're making. This will have water, leaven, flour and salt in it. Place it in a jar and put the jar in the fridge – this will become your next leaven. Three days prior to baking, begin feeding.

For more information about the pinch-of-dough method, see opposite.

- Use the fridge. Yeast and bacteria are most active at room temperatures, and they slow down in fridge temperatures. Some bakers will tell you not to put your leaven in the fridge, but those bakers are usually baking and refreshing their leaven every single day. But if you don't want to continually discard leaven and feed it every day, the fridge is your very best friend.

Halt it: If you're going away for four weeks or more, you can halt fermentation by placing your leaven in the freezer. First, discard half of the leaven and feed it. Be sure your jar has room for the leaven to expand, which it will do as it freezes.

When you return home, take the leaven out of the freezer and leave it at room temperature until it ferments; this will take no more than a day or two. Then use it as always to make your bread or put it in the fridge if you don't plan to bake for a few days.

LEAVEN MANAGED WITH THE PINCH-OF-DOUGH METHOD

My friend Ken bakes once a month for a farmers' market. He doesn't want his leaven to acidify between bakes, but he also doesn't want to have to discard and feed his leaven every day to reduce the acidity between bakes.

So, once a month, on the day of his bake, he mixes his dough ingredients (water, leaven, flour and salt), kneads and bulk ferments. At the dough division stage, Ken pinches off a piece of dough the size of a golf ball and places it in a jar and straight into the fridge, where he leaves it for a month.

Three days before the next bake, he removes the jar with the pinch of dough from the fridge and feeds it straight away with 75 g (2.65 oz) of wholemeal (whole-wheat) flour and enough cold water to make a firm paste. Then he feeds it every 12 hours (or after a full fermentation has occurred) leading up to the bake. As he is going to be baking hundreds of loaves, he doesn't discard with each feed but instead increases the overall leaven weight by increasing the amount of flour he adds to his leaven with each feed.

On the day of the bake, he has leaven for his monthly bake. At the dough division stage, once again he pinches off a piece of the new dough, and the whole process is repeated.

This leaven management method produces a leaven that sits in its own category. It isn't strong, it isn't medium strength, and it definitely isn't weak. It has no sourness and no gluten degradation. The method is great for people who bake infrequently and want to prevent their leaven from souring.

In case you're wondering, the salt in the pinch of dough that goes into the leaven causes no problems, as it's such a small amount.

Managing fermentation speed on baking day

Leaven fermentation speed on the day of the bake is determined by a number of factors: how you manage your leaven on the days leading up to the bake, how much leaven you use in the bake and the temperature of the room and ingredients you use on the day.

Slow it down: If you want a slower fermentation on baking day, you have several options, which you can use individually or in combination:

- Use cold water in your dough.
- Keep the room you're working in cool.
- Use the fridge.
- Use less leaven in your recipe (5% or 10%).
- Use a medium-strength or weak leaven.

Speed it up: If you want a faster fermentation on the day of the bake, the opposite options apply:

- Use warm water in your dough.
- Work in a warm room.
- Use a steamy warm oven (turned off) to speed up the bulk fermentation or the proof.
- Use more leaven in your recipe (20–40%, depending on the dough being made).
- Use a strong leaven.

For fast fermentation, you need one of the following types of leavens before the bake:

- a thin, liquid-like leaven, always kept at room temperature, discarded and fed twice a day and up to three times a day, every day
- a thick, firm, batter-like leaven, always kept at room temperature, discarded and fed once every day
- a thick, firm, batter-like leaven, always kept in the fridge and only brought to room temperature two or three days prior to a bake, and discarded and fed twice a day leading up to the bake
- a very dry leaven (a piece of dough from your previous bake), always kept in the fridge and only brought to room temperature three days before the bake, fed first to create a thick, firm batter, then discarded and fed once a day leading up to the bake.

Essentially, when a leaven is at room temperature, the number of required discards and feeds is higher than that needed for a leaven always kept in the fridge.

Remember to only discard and feed after fermentation has reached its peak, regardless of the instructions above. If your leaven hasn't reached peak fermentation and isn't on its way down, then wait, even if that means having to wait until the next day.

Leaven amounts

How much leaven you make before a baking day depends on how much bread you intend to make and the percentage of leaven you plan to use. In most cases, home bakers use 20% leaven in their recipes; that is, the weight of the leaven is 20% of the total weight of the flour used to make the bread. For example, a loaf with 20% leaven that uses 400 g (14 oz) flour needs 80 g (2.82 oz) leaven.

For information on how to weigh your leaven, see page 35.

As I've said, each time you use your leaven for baking bread, you should leave some of the leaven behind in the jar to kickstart the next leaven fermentation. If you're baking every few days or every day, consider leaving behind one-third of what you use for your regular bake. As a home baker, though, it's more likely that you'll be baking once a week, in which case you need to leave only a very small amount: a teaspoon is plenty.

Leaving a small amount of leaven behind like this will mean fermentation takes longer than it would in a larger amount, as there are comparatively fewer microorganisms available to ferment the next batch of flour added to your leaven.

If you find that your leaven has acidified too much for your liking, you can remove almost all of it, leaving behind only smears on the inside of your jar. The smears will be enough to start the next fermentation, and the acidity left behind will be completely diluted by your next feed.

MY LEAVEN

FLOURS

For my leaven, I work predominantly with wholegrain rye, because I love the big bubbles it creates in the leaven, and because it means all my breads have some wholegrain, regardless of what type of bread flour I'm using for the bulk of the dough.

However, if I'm getting ready to make a fluffy, super-light bread, such as panettone, I build a new, all white flour leaven, using one of the following methods:

- I refresh my rye leaven with only white bread flour and water.
- I grab a second jar, place a teaspoon of rye leaven in it and feed that leaven with only white flour and water.

By building a new leaven, I can keep my full-rye leaven available for my regular weekly bake.

CARING FOR MY LEAVEN

I feed my leaven only once a week, straight after using it to do a bake. I don't discard any leaven. The only leaven coming out of the jar is the leaven I'm using to make my bread.

When I feed my leaven, I create a thick, pancake-like batter with 150% hydration (remember I'm using wholegrain rye, which absorbs lots more water than white flour). It drops off a spoon, but not very easily. I put it in the fridge straight after it has been fed. I do this because I want to slow down leaven fermentation between bakes and to reduce the amount of acidity that accumulates in my leaven. I like my bread a bit sour, but not exceedingly sour.

To make sure I have made enough leaven for my usual bake, I keep a rubber band around my jar to show the height that the water and flour mixture should reach when I feed it if I want to make the same quantity again without weighing ingredients each time.

The only time I feed my leaven twice a day over multiple days is when I'm preparing it for an upcoming sourdough-baking class. Speed matters then, because the class would go for far too long if I used a medium-strength, slower leaven.

BAKING DAY

Generally, I bake between three and six loaves once a week. On my baking day, which is any day of the week when I realise we're low on bread, I take my leaven out of the fridge and bring it to room temperature. If I don't have time to bring it to room temperature, I use warm water (around 40°C / 105°F) to make my bread dough.

As my leaven is only fed once a week, it ferments the bread dough a little more slowly than a leaven managed for speed. My leaven takes around five hours to bulk ferment (at 20°C / 70°F) with a rise of one-third, while a strong leaven will take four hours at most.

STEP 2

Mix the ingredients

In this step

For more information

As with every other core step in the bread-baking process, when it comes to mixing ingredients, you can choose from various approaches. For example, the order in which you add your ingredients, the types of ingredients you choose to incorporate and the amounts you use are up to you. Be playful, knowing that every other baker is being playful too.

Ingredients

FLOUR

Flour is a key bread-baking ingredient, and therefore it's exciting to find out that there is a range of flours to play with. Each flour product performs differently. Rye, for example, is super-sticky when wet, while spelt feels incredibly smooth and soft, and high-gluten white flour is very stretchy and translucent. Each flour has a flavour all of its own, so don't hold back and be adventurous.

If you have trouble finding high-protein bread flour at your local supermarket, try your local wholefood store or a family-run food store. Even if they don't have any in stock, these types of stores are often very happy to order a new product in. Otherwise, there are many options to purchase online, or try visiting your favourite local sourdough bread bakery, asking them what flour they use and whether they're willing to sell some to you.

I also find word of mouth, including social media, a powerful tool for connecting with other bakers and tapping into local baking knowledge. Asking others for help is a community-building practice that makes people feel seen and valued. Before you know it, you'll have collected a fabulous group of baking friends along the way.

The list of possible extra ingredients in sourdough bread is endless.

FLOUR TYPES

White bread flour

White flour has become extremely popular as a major ingredient in baked goods of all kinds, because it produces very soft, light breads and pastries, due to its high content of gluten-forming proteins. It is made by removing the germ and bran (seed components) and is often bleached to increase whiteness: a practice that may lead to negative health impacts.

Compared to wholegrain (including wholemeal / whole-wheat) flours, white flour is nutritionally poor, with very low levels of fibre. However, when bread with a very open crumb is desired, white flour is predominantly used.

Wholegrain flours

Wholegrain (including wholemeal / whole-wheat) flours, unlike white flour, are nutritionally rich and fibre rich, because the grains' germ and bran have been retained. These flours produce a heavier loaf, as they contain fewer gluten-forming proteins. The germ and bran, in fact, act like scissors, cutting through the gluten strands responsible for supporting dough height during fermentation. Some bakers choose to do a one-hour autolyse or fermentolyse before kneading to improve gluten development when using wholegrain flours.

Ancient grains flours

Most wheat grains available today have been adapted through centuries of cultivation to meet the changing needs of societies. However, some grains, referred to as 'ancient', haven't been modified to the same extent as 'modern' wheat grains. These include einkorn, emmer, Khorasan and spelt. Once you've got the hang of baking with modern wheat varieties, I would encourage you to make bread with a variety of ancient grains, because each has its own nutritional profile, texture and flavour, allowing you to make a range of fantastic breads.

Freshly milled flours

I like to purchase ingredients in bulk as much as possible, and flour is no exception. But even though I bake frequently, having multiple large bags of flour in my pantry can mean they sit around for months, and flour has the potential to go rancid. When a seed is crushed to produce flour, that flour is completely exposed to oxidisation, speeding up the chemical changes that lead to rancidity.

To overcome this, I purchased a mill, stopped buying flour (with the exception of unbleached white flour) and started buying whole grains in bulk. Now I mill rye, spelt, wheat or emmer grain myself and use the freshly milled flour in my loaves. You can find out the protein content of grain you purchase in bulk by asking the company that sells it.

ADDING EXTRA GLUTEN

If you have difficulty sourcing high-protein flour, and your flour is particularly low in protein – anything under 11% – you can try using gluten flour (also called 'vital wheat gluten'), a flour-like powder that is gluten rich, to increase the strength of your flour. Gluten flour is added at the same time as the four key bread-making ingredients. Think of it simply as a flour that contains a high concentration of gluten.

While all gluten flours consist predominantly of gluten, they contain slightly varying amounts of protein, so look for the protein content on the packet to work out how to increase the gluten content of your existing flour by the correct amount. To keep the total weight of the flour used to make your dough the same, some of your regular flour needs to be substituted with the gluten flour.

Calculating how much flour and how much gluten flour you need is easier than you might think. All you need to start with are four numbers. When you have them, use them in the order given in the calculations below. On the right-hand side, there's an example to show how it works.

We'll say your regular flour has a protein content of 12%, and your gluten flour's is 80%. You want to achieve a protein content of 14%, and you're baking a loaf with a total flour weight of 400 g (the calculations work in exactly the same way with imperial weights). If you've calculated correctly, the results of equations 6 and 7 will add up to the total weight of flour that you started with.

THE NUMBERS YOU NEED	EXAMPLE
Your gluten flour's protein content (%)	80%
The required protein content for your loaf (%)	14%
Your regular flour's protein content (%)	12%
The total weight of flour you need for your loaf (g / oz)	400 g

CALCULATIONS			
1	(gluten flour protein) – (required protein) = A		80 – 14 = 66
2	(required protein) – (regular flour protein) = B		14 – 12 = 2
3	A + B = C		66 + 2 = 68
4	A ÷ C = D	= (proportion of regular flour required)	66 ÷ 68 = 0.97
5	B ÷ C = E	= (proportion of gluten flour required)	2 ÷ 68 = 0.03
6	D × (total flour weight)	= (weight of regular flour required)	0.97 × 400 = 388
7	E × (total flour weight)	= (weight of gluten flour required)	0.03 × 400 = 12

Flour amounts

The amount of flour you use to make a loaf of bread is informed by the size of the tin you will bake it in or the size of the proofing basket (banneton) you'll use to hold the dough's shape before baking. Getting the right flour weight for the size of tin or proofing basket is important. The correct flour weight for the tin or basket size will result in a properly sized dough: a dough that will rise adequately in the tin or proofing basket and produce a beautiful loaf of bread.

A dough too big for its tin or proofing basket will produce an underproofed (that is, under-fermented) dough, as you'll be forced to start baking prematurely to prevent the dough from spilling out of the tin.

A dough too small for its tin or proofing basket may trick you into thinking the dough hasn't risen enough, only for the resulting loaf to come out of the oven flat, as it overproofed (over-fermented) and had nothing left for the oven spring (the final rise, in the oven).

Bread tins: Most bread tins have a final loaf weight (or capacity weight) listed in their manufacturer's specifications, along with their dimensions. For example, a 680 g (1.5 lb) capacity tin is intended to hold a loaf weighing 680 g (1.5 lb). However, this final bread weight is completely geared towards mass-produced, super-light, non-sourdough bread. When I'm making a sourdough loaf for a 680 g (1.5 lb) tin, the flour weight alone is 700 g (24.7 oz), and the resulting baked loaf – regardless of flour type – weighs 1.2–1.3 kg (42–46 oz).

If I were to use less flour, the loaf would be far too small for this tin size. This illuminates just how much more bread you get when you make your own (or buy it from a sourdough bakery).

For more information about bread tins, see page 150.

Proofing baskets

Like bread tins, proofing baskets (bannetons) have a final loaf weight (or capacity weight) listed in their manufacturer's specifications. They are also sized by the internal diameter at the rim.

The same issues arise with manufacturers' capacity weights for proofing baskets: they aren't accurate for home-baked sourdough loaves. For example, manufacturers usually specify that a 20 cm (8 in) proofing basket can be used for a dough that weighs 550–750 g (19.4 oz–26.5 oz). But when I use this size of proofing basket, the flour alone weighs 550 g (19.4 oz).

For more information about proofing baskets, see page 151.

TROUBLESHOOTING A FLAT LOAF

Dianne asked me for advice because her breads always came out of the oven flat. She told me that the total flour weight for one of her loaves was 400 g (14 oz) and that she used a 450 g (1 lb) capacity tin.

Dianne would wait for the dough to reach the very top of the tin during the proofing stage before placing it in the oven, but the dough would flop the moment it hit the oven chamber.

I concluded that the dough size was too small for the tin. By the time the dough had risen to the top of this big tin, it was at its peak: fermentation had stopped, and there was none left for oven spring. Misled by the large tin size, Dianne was overproofing the dough. By increasing the size of her dough, Dianne was able to solve the problem.

For more information about oven spring, see page 164.

WATER

Water is an essential ingredient in the making of bread and plays many roles. It helps to combine all the ingredients together, it catalyses fermentation by activating amylase (the enzyme that helps bacteria and yeast break down complex carbohydrates into simple sugars), it gelatinises starches to produce a glistening crumb, and it helps dough remain pliable enough to expand during baking. High water amounts (high hydration) in doughs (combined with high-gluten, mostly white flours; excellent gluten development; high oven temperatures; and a steam-rich baking environment) produce open-crumb breads.

A range of water temperatures can be used when making bread: cold water if leaven or dough fermentation needs to be slowed down, and warm water if it needs to be sped up. A water temperature of 25–27°C (75–80°F) is often recommended; however, home bakers may at times choose to work with even warmer water temperatures, up to 35°C (95°F) or 40°C (105°F), as our homes are rarely as warm as a bakery, and the warmer water temperature can better support initial fermentation. The water cools down quickly once flour is added to it.

Chlorine in tap water can have an unpleasant smell and taste, but it won't kill the necessary bacteria in your leaven; it will only slow them down. If your tap water is heavily chlorinated, you can remove the chlorine before baking by filling a jug with the amount of water you need and allowing it to sit at room temperature overnight.

SALT

Salt helps in the development of the dough and adds flavour to the bread. There are lots of delicious salts to choose from. You can use table salt, sea salt, kosher salt or Himalayan pink salt. While salts might vary a little in flavour, the difference isn't always noticeable in bread, but the best way for you to find out is to give different salt products a go.

The finer the salt, the faster it's incorporated into the bread dough. Because the Baker's Percentage always works with weight, not volume, you won't run into the kinds of problems that can occur in volume-based cooking recipes. For example, a tablespoon of very fine salt will differ in weight from a tablespoon of coarse kosher salt, which could result in an over-salted or under-salted bread.

Iodised salt, which some people use to get a boost in dietary iodine, is perfectly fine for baking sourdough bread. I tend to avoid using table salts that contain anti-caking agents.

Salt can be added to leaven to slow its fermentation. But salt should not exceed 2% of the total leaven weight. When salt is added to leaven, it's a good idea to remember this, as you may want to reduce the salt amount added to your bread dough, to compensate for the salt present in the leaven.

As we've seen, for the Baker's Percentage, the salt weight is normally 2% of the total weight of the flour (regardless of the salt's coarseness or grain size). But if you're looking to reduce the salt in your diet, experiment with

using a lower salt percentage.
If you must avoid salt altogether, it is possible to make sourdough bread without any salt, but – to state the obvious – it will greatly affect the way your bread tastes. Salt also influences the way we experience the flavours of different flours, as it draws out their uniqueness. In addition, salt has an impact on gluten strength: it tightens it and therefore helps to support dough shape.

The right amount of salt (2% of the total flour weight) supports oven spring. Omitting salt leads to reduced overall oven spring but opens up the crumb a little. Too much salt, say 3%, can slow down fermentation speed and tighten the dough too much, reducing crumb size. If you happen to forget to add salt at the start, add it in during the kneading, so that you can spread it out as well as possible across the entire dough.

For more information about oven spring, see page 164.

EXTRA INGREDIENTS

There is an endless list of ingredients that can be included in sourdough bread, and once you have a good understanding of the basic bread-baking process, there are boundless recipes to play with.

Fruit bread has anywhere between 25% and 50% fruit, so if you find a fruit loaf you love and you want to replicate it at home, ask the baker what percentage of fruit they used, then at home translate that percentage into weights using the calculations in Chapter 5.

Dry ingredients like fruit and nuts can wick away water from the dough, reducing the amount of water available for gelatinisation of the crumb during baking. To prevent this, some bakers macerate the dry ingredients in water, juice, tea or alcohol for a few hours or overnight before mixing. As the macerated ingredients are full of water of their own as a result, they will no longer absorb water from the dough; in fact, they will contribute some extra liquid to it.

Maceration can also be used to introduce extra flavours, as dried fruit will absorb the flavours in the macerating liquid. When spices are to be added to a dough with macerated fruit and nuts – for example, in a spiced fruit loaf – they are added at the beginning, together with the flour and other core bread-baking ingredients (water, leaven and salt).

Some bakers take a different approach with dry ingredients: instead of macerating them, they make their dough slightly wetter, by increasing the hydration of the overall dough. This extra water initially creates a dough that is slightly too wet, but as the water is later absorbed by the dry ingredients, the end dough is just right in terms of hydration.

For information about incorporating extra ingredients, see page 106.

Hops Tea
4/24
Hops Tea
4/24
Oregano
02/23
Cinnamon
2022
Village Dreaming
Blackcurrant Jam
Village Dreaming
Boysenberry Gin
Japanese
Rice Tea
Elderberry Flowers
01/22
Calendula
2022
Mint
Jan 24
Lavender
02/2023
Oolong Tea
MAYAN CHILLI
CHOCOLATE
COTTAGE
Wild Apple Chai
Sage Honey
2021

Hops Tea
1/24
Lemon Grass
3/24
flower garden flower
Jan 24
Hawthorn Berry
2022
Lavender
Dec 2020
Village Dreaming
DRIED ROSEHIPS
Laurel
01/24
Laurel
01/24
Lemongrass
01/24
Laurel
01/24
Laurel
01/24

Mixing

When it comes to mixing, it's important to do it thoroughly. If you stop mixing too early, the dough will have small patches of dry flour everywhere, and its texture will be extremely rough.

The aim with mixing is to help the individual ingredients become one. Use it as a hand-strengthening exercise, and clench, squeeze and mix well. Alternatively, use a stand mixer.

ORDER OF ADDITION

There are two methods to choose from when it comes to the order in which you combine the four key ingredients in bread making, called 'autolyse' and 'fermentolyse'.

Autolyse

To follow the autolyse process, mix together the water and flour first, allow them to rest for 30 minutes, add the leaven and salt, then mix extremely well once more. Many commercial bakeries use this process, as it produces a smoother dough more quickly, reducing the time needed for kneading.

Fermentolyse

For home bakers, I recommend the fermentolyse method, but with salt also added (salt isn't usually added until after a fermentolyse). It's simple, it consists of fewer steps, and it requires a shorter baking day. It's the process I use.

To follow my fermentolyse process, simply put your water, leaven, salt and flour (in that order) in a bowl, mix them together, then allow them to rest in the bowl for 30 minutes. With this method, fermentation begins the moment the ingredients are mixed together.

INCORPORATING EXTRA INGREDIENTS

Additional ingredients, such as dried fruit, nuts, seeds and sprouted grains, can be added at various points of the bake. Knowing what is possible gives you options, and options give you flexibility. Below are your options; be playful and try them all, because each one produces excellent results.

At the very beginning

Add the extra ingredients at the very beginning, at the same time as you combine the four key ingredients. The upside to adding them at this point is twofold: first, you are reducing steps (which, for a home baker, is usually helpful); and second, it's easy to mix additional ingredients evenly through your dough at this stage.

If you're adding fruits at the very start of your dough making and want them to keep their integrity and shape, don't use a machine mixer – especially if the fruits have been macerated. The dough hook will completely squish them, compromising both the fruit and some of the gluten's ability to build the dough's structure.

Instead, mix by hand, then knead by hand, using stretch and folds, coil folds or the Rubaud method of kneading. Don't use palm kneading, as this too will crush the fruits.

For kneading instructions, see page 120.

During kneading

Introduce extra ingredients during kneading, after the four key ingredients have been mixed and rested. Add them incrementally with each stretch and fold (or another repeated action) to get an even distribution.

During shaping

Incorporate extra ingredients during shaping, between the bulk fermentation and the proofing. Stretch out and flatten the dough, then add the extra ingredients incrementally as you fold the dough into two or three layers. Then, to achieve an even better spread, palm knead the dough a little. One way to incorporate fruit for a boule (round loaf) during shaping is as follows:

1. Stretch out the dough on the benchtop to create a large rectangle and spread some of the fruit across the rectangle.
2. Grab one end of the dough and fold it halfway, to the middle of the rectangle, then take hold of the same end again and fold it in the same direction, to meet the edge of the dough. By this stage, you will have created a long, folded rectangle with several layers of fruit.
3. Stretch this rectangle to create more length, spread the remaining fruit across the middle of it, then fold each end of the dough into the middle.
4. Tuck the edges of the dough under all the way round, then drag and rotate the dough across the benchtop, continuing to tuck under the edges, to create tension and a boule shape.

For more information about shaping, see page 138.

HOW I MIX MY INGREDIENTS

I use a fermentolyse rest after mixing the key ingredients. When I'm mixing them in my stand mixer, I put the water in the bowl first, because my mixer doesn't do well if I start with the flour. I then add leaven, salt and the flour last. And when I'm hand mixing, I find having the water as the bottom layer in the bowl, once again, helps me, as it allows me to spread the leaven and salt, which are added next, more evenly, before the flour is added and all the ingredients are mixed. And as previously stated, I always add salt in the fermentolyse, to reduce steps.

I prefer to add additional ingredients such as sesame seeds, pumpkin seeds (pepitas) and sunflower seeds at the very beginning, at the same time as my key ingredients and before the fermentolyse rest, simply because, once again, it reduces steps and allows them to be easily incorporated and spread.

However, if I'm making an enriched bread, such as a panettone or a fruit bread that involves macerating the fruit, I add the macerated fruit incrementally, either during stretch-and-fold kneading, with each fold, or in layers at the shaping stage.

STEP 3

Rest the dough

In this step

This is the first rest, and it occurs right after you mix together the four key ingredients if you're using the fermentolyse process with salt (which I recommend) or just the flour and water if you're following the autolyse process.

Reasons for resting

A major rest always occurs straight after flour and water (autolyse) or flour, water, leaven and, in this book, salt (fermentolyse) are mixed together. This rest typically lasts 30 minutes, but it can last up to one hour when you're using a high proportion of wholegrain flour. The purposes of the rest are to allow the flour to get fully wet, starting the development of gluten, and to give that gluten time to 'relax', which is what we need for stretchiness in the dough and structure in the final loaf. After the rest, you'll find a dough that's easy to stretch during kneading.

Later in the process, after the dough has been divided, a bench rest makes final shaping easier. In fact, every time the dough starts to get a bit sticky and hard to work with, give it a rest, and when you come back to it, it will have firmed up and be much easier to handle.

With 'no-knead' doughs with high-gluten flours (13% or more), bakers use time, lots of it, and high hydrations to develop gluten in the dough by simply resting it. As I've mentioned, in this book, all the recipes and examples include salt in the fermentolyse, because not including salt at this stage adds an extra step for a home baker and can often lead to salt being forgotten altogether. The inclusion of the salt does not negate the purposes of resting.

Resting allows the flour to get fully wet, starts gluten development and gives gluten time to 'relax'.

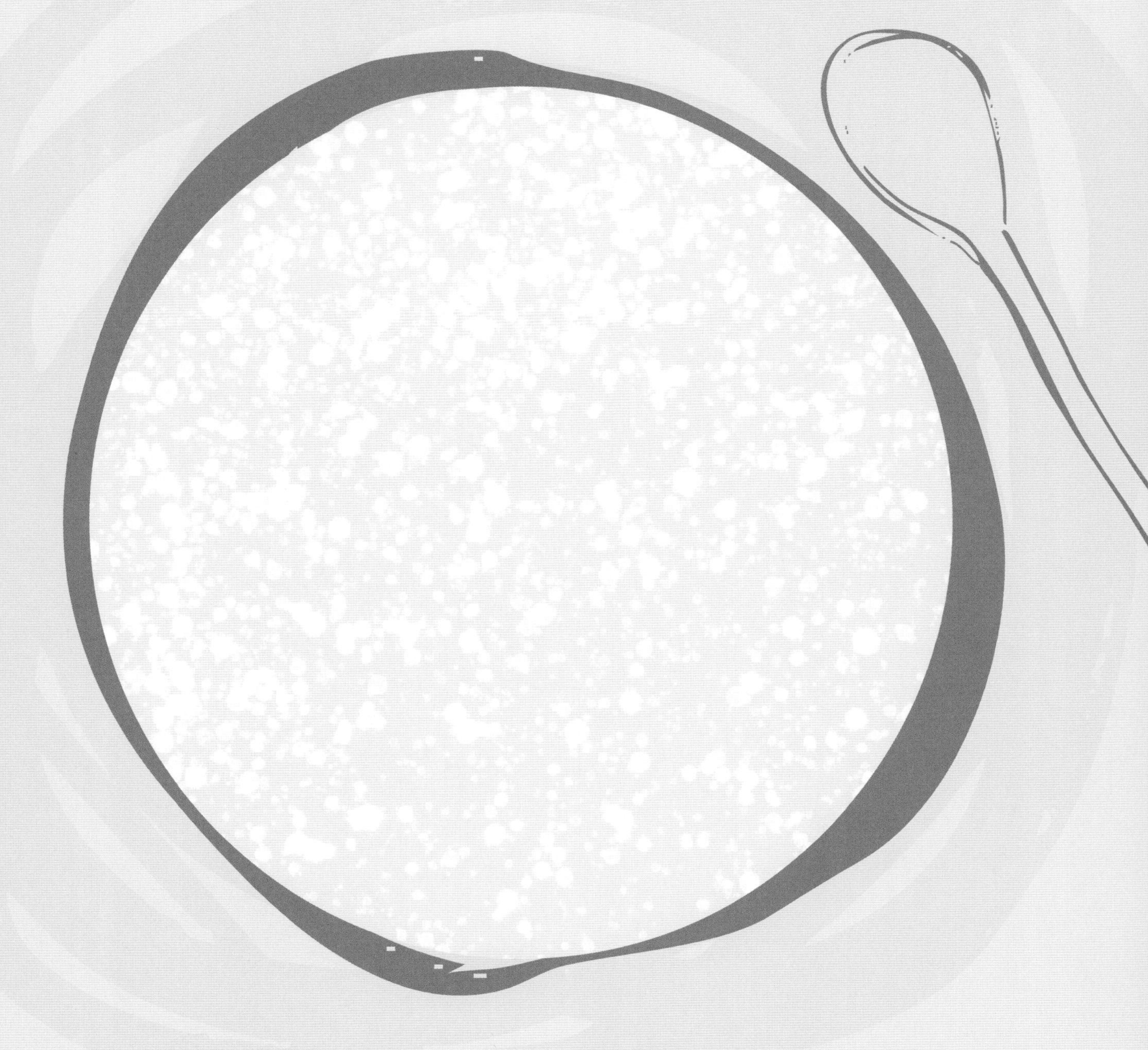

Timing adjustments

The rest after mixing is usually about 30 minutes long, and it's good practice to stick to this amount of time. As a home baker, however, you can choose to shorten the rest that follows the mixing to as little as 15 minutes, to fit bread making around your other commitments. Keep in mind that if the rest is shorter, more kneading will be required later.

The motivation for choosing one or the other option for resting time is all about you. One day you might want to do six kneading sessions of four stretch and folds with six 30-minute rests to keep you company, and another day you might want to get the kneading done and out of the way as soon as possible, with more kneading per session and fewer and shorter dough rests. You have choice.

If your fermentolyse rest is longer than 30 minutes, just remember that fermentation began the moment the leaven was added, so the dough will have been fermenting throughout the resting time. And it will continue to ferment during kneading. This is important to note if you choose to spread out the kneading with frequent long rests between each knead, as you should handle the dough more gently (don't palm knead), especially when you get to the last few kneading sessions. If you're using a strong leaven and spread kneading out over three or four hours, the bulk fermentation will most likely have occurred by the time of the final knead. For a beginner baker, extending the kneads and rests over three hours can make it hard to discern when the bulk fermentation is complete (that one-third rise). Kneading over a much shorter period of time gives the dough an undisturbed rise that can be easily observed. However, if you choose to extend the kneads and rests over several hours and you're not sure whether the dough has risen by a third, look for a smooth, cohesive dough, soft to the touch, billowy, and not sticking to the inside of its container.

STEP 4

Feed your leaven

In this step

For more information

Leaven is lovely company, I think, and great fun to manage. It is a living thing; this is why it feels to me like I have a friend in the kitchen. It is also a very simple thing: flour mixed with water and left to ferment.

Fermentation is almost inevitable once flour becomes adequately wet. In fact, bacteria and yeasts are lounging on the surface of the flour very much hoping you'll add water to it.

As we've seen, leaven is an essential raising agent in all bread baking, and bread won't rise without it. So feed your leaven straight after you use it on baking day; that way it can't be forgotten, ensuring the leaven isn't unintentionally left out for hours, acidifying, as you focus on making your next loaf of bread.

Ingredients

FLOUR

You can be strategic with the flour you use to feed your leaven. Use only high-gluten white flour if you want nothing short of a very open crumb and a very soft, lofty bread.

Alternatively, use high-gluten white flour mixed with a small amount of wholegrain flour if your leaven is a bit inactive and needs a higher level of nutrition (as wholegrain is rich in nutrients). Or try making a 100% spelt, rye, emmer or Khorasan leaven.

By creating leavens with different types of flours, you can make richly flavoured doughs and doughs with a higher proportion of wholegrain and, therefore, nutrition.

Feed your leaven right after you use it.

WATER

If you don't plan to bake for more than two days, use cold water. If you plan to bake the next day, use warm water (25°C / 75°F).

Making the correct amount

When you feed your leaven, you will want to ensure you have made enough for the next bake.

Your jar will contain a small amount of leaven left over from today's bake. Let's say you'll need 200 g (7 oz) of leaven for your next bake. The easiest way to achieve this is to simply weigh out 200 g (7 oz) of your chosen flour and mix it into enough water to create either a thick, firm batter or a medium or thin batter, depending on how firm or liquid-like you want your leaven to be. This will produce more leaven than you need, but it will work for all flour types.

As you get to know each flour type and the amount of water it can absorb, you will be able to produce an amount of leaven that is closer to the actual amount you need.

When you've made the same bread several times and know the exact amount of leaven you need, including the leftover amount that will remain in the jar, then, rather than weighing the flour each time you feed your leaven, you can just use a rubber band around your leaven jar. Position it to show the height of the leaven prior to fermentation, and when you next feed it, if you have added flour and water to the height of that rubber band, you'll know you have enough leaven for your next bake.

Storing leaven

If you don't plan to bake every day, store the refreshed leaven in the fridge. If you plan to bake the next day, keep the leaven out of the fridge, at room temperature.

STEP 5

Knead the dough

In this step

For more information

The purpose of kneading is to *develop gluten*. Gluten is the building material of bread, giving dough its stretchiness and bread its structure. Kneading stretches the gluten in the dough to form a kind of web, increasing the dough's strength. That's gluten development.

When you discover that to develop gluten you simply need to stretch the dough, you also realise that there's no wrong way to knead. While some kneading techniques are better suited to some doughs than others, in most cases, as long as you are stretching the dough and stretching it for long enough for the gluten to fully develop, then all is extremely well in the kneading world. This explains why there are so many different kneading techniques. Later in this step, I'll describe some of the most common kneading techniques – plus one of my own – so you can experiment and find your favourites.

The aim of kneading

Whichever kneading technique you use, the goal is the smoothest dough possible with the type of flour you're using. Smoothness and dough strength come from either lots of kneading or lots of dough rests between a handful of kneads.

In other words, we have an inverse relationship here. If you want to get the kneading (and the gluten development that follows) over and done with in one or two bursts over a short period of time – 30 minutes, for example – then knead lots. If you want to reduce the amount of kneading you do, then give the dough lots of resting time and knead over a period of up to three hours, with 30-minute rests in between.

The smoothest dough will be the dough made with pure white flour. This is a

Aim for the smoothest dough possible.

smooth, shiny, almost translucent dough that loses its stickiness along the way. It can stretch extremely well when moderate hydrations (around 75%) are used to make it; it can hold its shape and peels away from the side of the bowl rather than taking the shape of the bowl like a liquid. When very high hydrations are used (80% and above), the dough will stretch even further, allowing you to make breads such as ciabatta, focaccia and pan de cristal.

The least smooth dough will be dough made using wholegrain flours. This is always less shiny and more sticky than predominantly white dough, but it too starts to peel away from the bowl when well kneaded, becomes stronger over time and is able to hold its shape.

There's one exception: a dough made completely with rye flour will never look smooth, no matter how much you knead it. There's very little gluten in rye flour – so little, in fact, that you can't develop it. The dough will be really sticky and will stay sticky. Essentially, you can only ever mix this dough, as it's impossible to stretch. Work the dough using either slap and folds or palm kneading to ensure it's mixed well.

For information on kneading techniques, see pages 120–6.

Kneading amounts

HOW MUCH?

In this book, I'm trying to give clear directions, to get you started with sourdough bread baking. However, it's difficult to give instructions on how much kneading your dough requires, because the way you handle dough is extremely subjective. Everyone handles dough so very differently. One person will pull hard on it and fold it in with force. Another will pull and fold gently. The development of the dough will vary between these two people, even if they complete the same amount of kneading.

So, there are countless possible variations when it comes to how much you should knead your dough. When you become aware of these variations, you'll understand why observation is key to bread making.

And I can't emphasise enough how important it is to take a good look at your dough *before* you start kneading: it is a vital observation to inform you when to stop kneading. Notice the dough's rough texture. You want that rough texture to completely disappear. You're looking for the smoothest dough possible, whether it's made from mostly white, a mixture of white and wholegrain, or all wholegrain flours. Can you over-knead? This is rarely, if ever, a concern. In most cases, home bakers under-knead their doughs; if in doubt, knead more – especially for free-form loaves, as these rely on excellent gluten development.

HOW MANY?

Just as there are several ways to knead dough, there are several approaches to how many times to knead it. Some bakers do all their kneading at once, after the initial dough rest. Others will knead twice, three times – even up to six times – with rests in between.

Each time you start kneading, the dough will be easy to stretch. Then, not long after, it will become harder to stretch. This is because dough becomes stronger in just a few kneads. When you're kneading by hand, it can seem counterintuitive to keep working the dough when it starts to pull back in this way. This is one of the reasons that some bakers knead a little, then rest the dough, then knead a little more, then rest again. The rests tend to reduce the overall kneading required but spread it out over a longer period.

Resting durations vary too, from five minutes to 30 minutes.

Some of the decisions around kneading can be based on what else you have going on during the day. If you're looking for a reason to leave your desk while working from home, spread your kneading out, spacing short bursts through the entire bulk fermentation. On the other hand, if you need to get the kneading done in a concise time block, knead only once, extremely well.

TWO INVARIABLES

Having said all that, once you've become experienced with different types of doughs and baking methods, if you're relatively consistent in your kneading style, you'll discover there are two kneading invariables:

- When baking bread in a tin, you can get away with doing far less kneading than when making free-form bread.
- Higher-hydration doughs must be kneaded for longer than lower-hydration doughs.

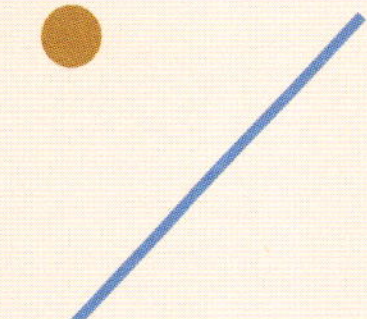

THE WINDOWPANE TEST

Use this simple observation when you're using predominantly white flour and want to know how much more kneading is required. (The test works poorly with wholegrain flours.)

After a dough rest (never straight after kneading), pinch off a piece of dough about the size of a golf ball. Lightly wet your fingers and use the fingertips of both hands to gently stretch the dough outwards, rotating it after each gentle stretch. You're aiming to stretch it until it measures about 10 cm × 10 cm (4 in × 4 in) and is extremely thin, so it becomes transparent, like a windowpane. If the dough stretches well and forms a thin pane, you'll know the gluten in the dough is well developed and you've done enough kneading.

Kneading techniques

Every time a new kneading technique becomes popular, it can be tempting to think that it's the best way to develop gluten. But if you're having difficulty getting adequate gluten development in your doughs, it won't be because of the kneading technique you're using; it will be because you're not kneading enough.

Therefore, it's important to choose a kneading method that suits you. Remember: all methods of stretching dough develop gluten.

Some home bakers use two or three different kneading techniques for each single loaf of bread, but most of the time it's also perfectly fine to use only one. At a basic level, as long as you knead enough, the results will be the same. But you will find that some kneading approaches are better suited to a particular dough than others and that sometimes using a combination of kneading techniques can help you.

You will also find that some kneading techniques, such as the lamination fold and coil fold (see pages 124 and 123), can be deployed after the bulk fermentation and during the preshape to help you further develop the gluten strength in your dough prior to final shaping.

And if you're not up to hand kneading or just don't fancy it some days, you can always use a machine mixer with a dough hook attached, as it will produce an equally beautiful dough.

There are a few things to consider when kneading, regardless of kneading technique:

- Cleaning the benchtop is always a great way to approach kneading, even if you are kneading inside a bowl.
- Wash your hands well and remove hand and wrist jewellery, as it will get in the way and caught up in your dough.
- Don't dust your hands with flour, because you don't want to introduce more flour into the dough, and once you start dusting your hands, benchtop or dough with flour, you'll find you want to keep doing so. Instead, prepare yourself for stickiness; that stickiness will eventually disappear (unless you're working with rye flour).
- It is extremely important to let the dough rest after a knead, because it's after a rest that you can discern how well the dough has been kneaded. If you try to assess gluten development via a windowpane test straight after the dough has been kneaded, the dough will break. Rest the dough for 15 minutes, then check how well it stretches.
- If in doubt, knead more.

STRETCH AND FOLD

Leave the dough in the bowl. Use one hand to hold and turn the bowl and the other to stretch the dough.

Reach underneath and to one side of the dough at the far side of the bowl and stretch the dough out as far as it will go. It doesn't matter if it breaks. To achieve maximum stretch, wiggle the dough from side to side as you pull on it; the wiggle motion forces the dough to stretch both horizontally and vertically. Then fold the stretch back into the dough by pushing it down onto the side closest to you.

With each completed stretch and fold, turn the bowl just enough to allow you to grab another part of the dough, then repeat until all sides of the dough have been worked.

If you are working with a small amount of dough, after a few stretches the whole dough will want to come out of the bowl when you try to stretch it. When this happens, let gravity create the stretch as you dangle the dough above the bowl, then push the dough down to complete the fold. Alternatively, use a different kneading technique.

SLAP AND FOLD

Tip the dough onto your benchtop. Don't dust the bench or dough with flour. Using both hands with palms facing up, position a hand on either side of the dough towards the edge that is furthest from you. Slip the fingertips of each hand beneath the dough towards each other.

Lift the dough off the benchtop with palms facing you, so that most of the dough is hanging down below your hands.

Keeping hold of the dough throughout, flick the hanging part of the dough away from you and allow it to fall straight down to the benchtop, landing it with a slap.

Take the edge you're holding over to meet the edge furthest away from you, creating a fold.

Rotate the dough by 90 degrees and repeat until all parts of the dough have been worked.

COIL FOLD

Using both hands with palms facing up, position a hand on either side of the dough and halfway across it. Slip the fingertips of each hand beneath the dough towards each other.

Lift both hands upwards with palms facing you, stretching the dough while it hangs over your hands.

Without adjusting your hold, move the dough a little to bring both of the hanging ends to sit roughly below your hands. Then drop the part of the dough you're holding onto the ends, creating a loose coil in the dough.

Rotate the dough by 90 degrees and repeat until all parts of the dough have been worked.

THE 'NO-KNEAD' METHOD

This method, which is also called the 'unloaf' method, should literally require no kneading, but in reality, almost every baker who promotes 'no-knead' recipes is, in fact, kneading to some extent. Every time the dough is handled and something is done to it that involves it being stretched, a knead is occurring, because even shaping is kneading.

It's important to clarify: you can make bread to be baked in a tin with minimal kneading, but the word here is 'minimal'; it's not 'no' knead. If you stretch dough in any way, even by giving it a good mix, then you're kneading.

LAMINATION FOLD

This kneading technique can only be used after considerable gluten development has already occurred; in the absence of adequate gluten strength, it's impossible to achieve. You can use the lamination fold as both a kneading technique and a final-shaping technique.

It can be extremely useful when extra gluten development is required, when fruits or nuts are added to a dough or when a very high hydration dough is being made. Learning this technique will also have you making your own filo pastry.

The goal is to create a very wide, thin film of dough in the shape of a rectangle, like a huge windowpane.

Using a spray bottle, spray the benchtop with a thin film of water.

Tip the dough onto the benchtop and use both hands to work around the dough, stretching out a small portion of the edge of the dough at a time. Work with one hand above the dough, stretching, and with the other hand below the dough, palm up, supporting the stretch.

Complete each stretch by gently pressing the dough down onto the benchtop. The moist benchtop surface will grip the dough and hold the stretch in place. Use the spray bottle to keep your hands lightly moist.

When you've stretched the dough around its whole circumference, fold it up like a business letter, in thirds, bringing the two outer thirds, one at a time, over the middle third with light fingertip movements.

With the resulting narrow rectangle of dough, repeat the two business-letter folds.

In total, you should make four folds in the dough, resulting in a neat rectangular package.

ACCORDION FOLK FOLD

This is one of my own kneading creations. Lift the whole of the dough in both hands. Stretch it out to the left and right simultaneously, then relax it back in – as if you're playing an accordion.

Repeat the stretch and relax several times, all the while singing Italian folk songs. It sounds like I'm being silly, but it is indeed another way of stretching dough. If you prefer the gym to Italian folk songs, think of it as a chest expander.

RUBAUD METHOD

This is a beautiful technique. Leaving the dough in the bowl, use a scooping motion, slipping your fingertips underneath the far edge of the dough and lifting it slightly in a gentle stretch, before dropping it back down. Imagine you're simply loosening the dough away from the side of the bowl.

Repeat this motion quickly and smoothly, turning the bowl regularly, so you work your way around all of the dough.

PALM KNEADING

Holding the edge of the kitchen benchtop with your non-dominant hand, put the heel of your other hand into the centre of the dough and push it away from you across the benchtop.

Now, with the pushing hand, grip the far edge and pull the dough back over itself to create a fold.

Rotate the dough a little and repeat the push and fold until all parts of the dough have been worked.

As you practise this, you'll find you can create a wonderful, seamless, fluid, looping movement.

MACHINE MIXING

Machine mixing is an excellent way to develop gluten strength in your dough and often a necessary tool when making brioche or panettone dough. And for home bakers wanting to work predominantly with high-gluten white flour and very high hydrations, of 80% or more, machine mixing makes that extremely easy.

Having said that, please rest assured that you can achieve the same level of gluten development for non-enriched doughs with hand kneading; the machine is simply less work.

Use your machine's dough hook to mix the dough and to knead it. At first, have the machine knead the dough slowly, to help the ingredients combine a little more after an autolyse or fermentolyse. Then speed it up a little, to get further gluten development occurring. At the very end, you may want to speed up the kneading even further for about ten seconds, to force the dough completely away from the bowl's side.

During the kneading, you will at first observe the dough spread across the bottom of the bowl, flat and sticking to the inside of the bowl. After a few minutes of machine mixing, the dough will start to peel away a little from the bowl. After further kneading, it will peel away even more, until it is entirely centred around the dough hook and no longer interested in the side of the bowl. It's a great way to discern gluten development as it happens.

One factor to be aware of is dough temperature. If the dough is mixed too fast for too long, it can become hot and almost liquid-like. Let the dough rest between machine kneads if you see it's getting too hot: the bowl will start to feel very warm, or a food thermometer will show the dough to be around 30°C (85°F).

A BAKING SCHEDULE FOR TIN BREAD WITH MULTIPLE KNEADS

Carlo works from home. He bakes once every two weeks and likes to spread out his kneads as welcome breaks from his desk. He uses a Baker's Percentage formula that requires the leaven weight to be 20% of the total flour weight.

1. 10 am – Prepare a leaven. Carlo takes the leaven out of the fridge. Instead of bringing it to room temperature, he's going to use water at 40°C (105°F) for the dough mix, to kick-start fermentation.

2. Mix the ingredients. Carlo adds the ingredients to a large bowl in this order: warm water, leaven, salt and flour. He mixes them very well, until he's certain there are no dry patches of flour.

3. 10.20 am – Rest the dough. He covers the bowl containing the dough with another, inverted bowl and leaves it to rest for 30 minutes.

4. Feed your leaven. Carlo feeds his leaven, making it thick (80% hydration, white flour) to mitigate the two-week gap between bakes. He puts it back in the fridge.

5. 10.50 am – Knead the dough. Carlo starts kneading. He does four kneads in total, separated by 15-minute rests. Each knead consists of four stretch and folds. The dough stays in the bowl throughout and is covered during rests.
   For kneading instructions, see page 121.

6. 12 pm – Bulk ferment the dough. After the fourth knead, Carlo greases the interior of a transparent rectangular food container with a lightly flavoured olive oil. He places the dough inside and pushes it down to create a roughly even surface, making sure there are no gaps between the container and the dough. He seals the lid and marks the level of the top of the dough with masking tape on the outside of the container.

7. 4 pm – Final shape the dough. After four hours, the dough has risen by one-third of its original height. As Carlo is only making one loaf and is baking it in a tin, he doesn't need to divide or preshape the dough. He places the dough on the benchtop and does the final shaping so that it will fit easily into the tin.
   For final-shaping instructions, see page 142.

8 **Transfer the dough.** Carlo greases the bread tin with olive oil and places the dough inside it.

9 **4.10 pm – Proof the dough.** Carlo makes the oven steamy by placing a tray on the oven floor and filling it with boiling water. He puts the tin containing the dough onto the top shelf in the oven and closes the door.

Carlo's friend calls to invite him out for dinner. He'll need to leave in about an hour's time to get to the restaurant. Carlo is excited to go but realises he'll need to slow down the dough's proofing by using the fridge. However, he'll let the dough proof in the oven until he leaves, to ensure fermentation is occurring.

5.40 pm Carlo checks the fridge temperature is set to 4°C (40°F). He takes the bread tin containing the dough from the oven, places it inside a plastic bag, seals the bag, then puts it into the fridge.

He tops up the water in the tray on the oven floor. When the oven heats up later, it will create humidity inside the oven.

Finally, he leaves a note for his housemate asking them to turn the oven on to 250°C (475°F) at 7.45 pm.

'*Arrivederci*,' he says and leaves the house to ride into town.

10 **8.30 pm – Bake the bread.** Carlo has just got home. He takes the tin containing the proofed dough out of the fridge and puts it straight into the oven.

11 **9.05 pm Cool the bread.** Carlo checks the bread is cooked, by looking for a beautiful golden colour all over, then skewers the bread with a food thermometer to check it has reached 95°C (203°F). It has, and therefore he removes it from the oven. The loaf has risen beautifully, with a full oven spring.

Carlo is happy. Tomorrow at breakfast, he and his housemate will enjoy the delicious loaf he made.

STEP 6

Bulk ferment the dough

In this step

For more information

Bulk fermentation is the first fermentation stage in bread making, for which the entire dough – the bulk – is kept together.

The bulk fermentation can occur after kneading or in parallel with kneading. For the latter, you break up the kneading into short bursts with rests in between. A gentle kneading method, such as a stretch and fold or coil fold (see pages 121 and 123), is best for this approach, as it prevents the bubbles in your dough from getting squished.

Measuring the rise

When you're starting out with bulk fermentation, it's easiest to put the dough into a lightly oiled, straight-sided, transparent food container, mark its height and then watch it rise. Aim for an increase of one-third of its original height and no more.

For a long time, I tried to discern the fermentation rise of my doughs while they fermented in a round bowl. It's easiest to mix the ingredients in round bowls, but their shape, with the widest part at the top, means the dough spreads out a lot. This makes it difficult for beginners to judge the true height increase.

Over time, you'll become more and more confident with the bulk fermentation. You'll be able to make observations that will allow you to leave the dough in a round bowl and know without measuring when it's time to divide and shape. For example, you'll see how the dough becomes billowy and puffed up, softer and smoother. When you peel the dough away from the side of the bowl, you'll feel how it releases easily without sticking to your fingers or the bowl.

The dough becomes billowy and puffed up, softer and smoother.

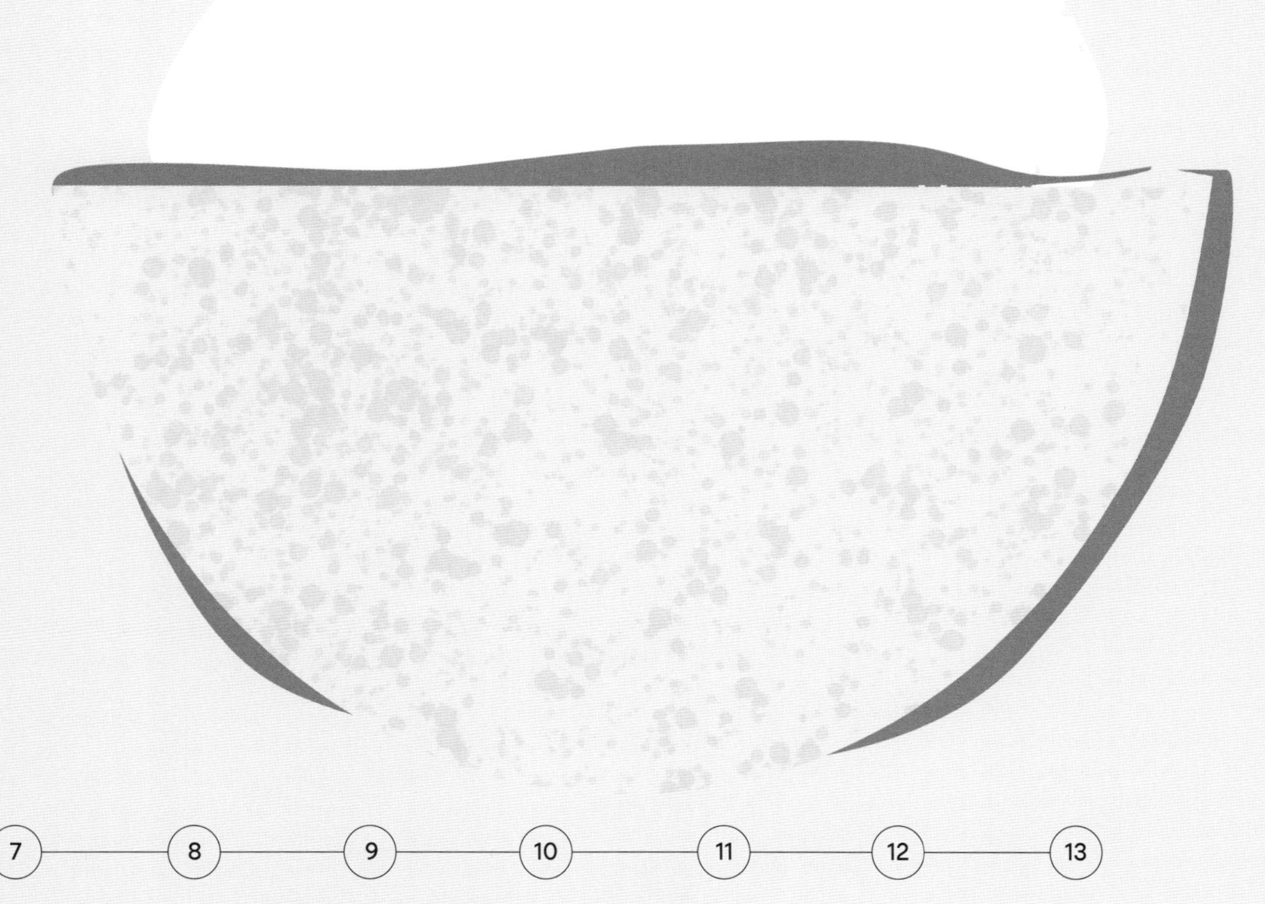

However, if you want to speed up your understanding of bulk fermentation, I highly recommend you use a straight-walled, clear food container to do so. It's also much easier to store the dough covered in the fridge in a straight-walled container with a lid than in a round bowl.

Controlling fermentation speed

As a home baker, you will sometimes want to change the speed of the bulk fermentation so you can fit in other daily tasks and outings. You may be in a hurry to go out to meet a friend and you need to make the fermentation happen quickly. Or, somewhere along the bulk fermentation, you may remember you have a dance class, choir gathering or winter swim at the lake and need to slow down your dough's fermentation. Both options are open to you.

SPEED IT UP

Your oven is the perfect place for speeding up bulk fermentation when you need to do so.

Leaving the oven switched off, place a large tray or dish capable of holding liquid on the oven floor.

Bring the kettle to the boil, then carefully pour water from the kettle into the tray, making sure it doesn't overflow.

Close the oven door, leave it for 15 minutes, then check the temperature of the oven with an oven thermometer placed on the rack you intend to put the dough container on. Don't use an infrared thermometer, as it will only give you the temperature of the oven walls or floor, as opposed to the air temperature.

The oven will have become warm and humid. A temperature anywhere between 25°C and 30°C (75°F and 85°F) is great. If it's much warmer than 30°C (85°F), open the oven door to cool it down a little. Eventually, you won't need to check the temperature of the oven, as you will have worked out how much boiling water and which tray produce the best oven temperature for the bulk fermentation.

THE ALIQUOT JAR METHOD

If for some reason you can't put your entire dough into a transparent container for the bulk fermentation, the aliquot jar method can contribute, to some extent, to an understanding of how fermentation is progressing in your dough.

You simply pinch off a small piece of dough, half the size of a golf ball, put it into a glass jar (or clear, straight-walled container) and observe it as fermentation proceeds. When it has increased by one-third, it can give you a sense of how your bulk fermentation is tracking. I use the word 'sense', because, although you'll come across the technique in bread-making resources, it's not an accurate way of discerning bulk fermentation.

The challenge with this assessment is that the small piece of dough will be affected by temperature changes more quickly than the bulk of the dough. For example, on a very warm day, the small piece of dough will heat up and therefore ferment faster than the mass.

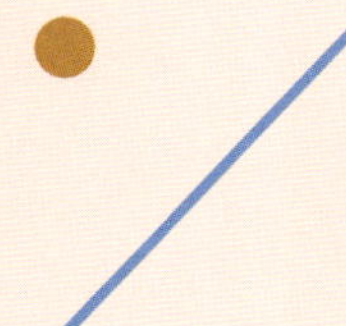

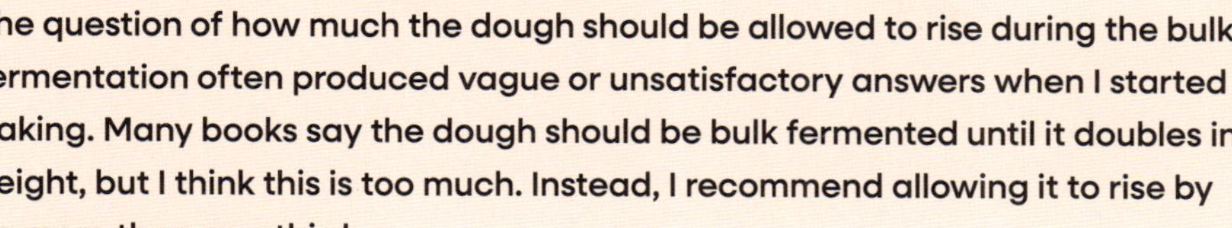

SHOULDN'T THE DOUGH DOUBLE IN HEIGHT?

The question of how much the dough should be allowed to rise during the bulk fermentation often produced vague or unsatisfactory answers when I started baking. Many books say the dough should be bulk fermented until it doubles in height, but I think this is too much. Instead, I recommend allowing it to rise by no more than one-third.

When you consider that the dough needs to rise twice – once during the bulk fermentation and again during proofing – and that it is fermenting from the moment you add leaven, and all the way through dividing and shaping, you realise it's too much to want it to double at the first fermentation. By the time the dough is at proofing stage, it will be running out of fermenting strength.

When the oven temperature is at 25–30°C (75–85°F), place the container of dough in the oven for as long as it needs, removing it from the oven once it has risen by one-third.

SLOW IT DOWN

You can slow down bulk fermentation by using the fridge. First, though, let the dough ferment for about 30 minutes at room temperature. Putting it straight into the fridge before it shows any signs of fermentation can slow down the fermentation too much.

After 30 minutes, cover the dough to stop it drying out, if it's not already in a sealed container, then place it in the fridge.

You can leave the dough in the fridge for a few hours or overnight, but note that while the fridge slows fermentation down, it doesn't stop it. So, don't leave dough in the fridge for too long, or it will over-ferment: it will rise by more than one-third.

When it suits you to speed up fermentation again, simply take the dough back out of the fridge.

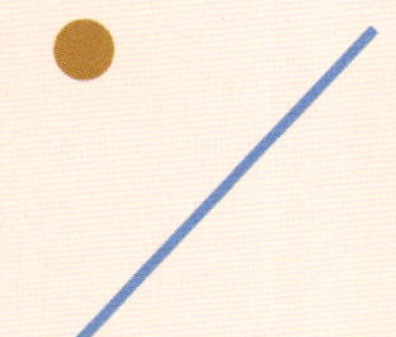

ADDING FLAVOUR WITH COLD BULK FERMENTATION

We saw earlier that you can add flavour to your sourdough bread by using a strong-flavoured leaven. An alternative method is to allow the dough to ferment in the fridge. This can be done during the first (bulk) or second (proofing) fermentation. The extra flavour comes from slowing down fermentation, causing more sourness to be produced in the dough by bacteria and yeasts.

If you're a beginner baker, however, keep in mind that it's much easier to observe fermentation occurring with the dough at room temperature than when it's out of sight in the fridge.

A BAKING SCHEDULE FOR LONG BULK FERMENTATION

Paula bakes one tin loaf of bread once a week and feeds her leaven on bake day. She works away from home during the day. She chooses a Baker's Percentage leaven formula of 5% relative to the total flour weight. The low leaven percentage means the bulk fermentation happens very slowly, while she's at work. Paula loves to bake in the evening when she gets home.

1. 6 am – Prepare a leaven. Paula removes her leaven from the fridge to bring it to room temperature. Then she makes breakfast and gets ready for work.

2. 7 am – Mix the ingredients. To a large bowl she adds, in this order, room-temperature water, leaven, salt and flour. She mixes them together well, making sure there are no patches of dry flour.

3. 7.20 am – Rest the dough. Paula covers the bowl containing the dough with a plate and leaves it to rest for 30 minutes.

4. Feed your leaven. Paula feeds her leaven and puts it straight back in the fridge.

5. 7.50 am – Knead the dough. Paula kneads the dough, doing 30 stretch and folds.
   For kneading instructions, see page 121.

6. 8 am – Bulk ferment the dough. Paula greases a transparent rectangular food container with a lightly flavoured olive oil, places the dough inside, squishes it down and seals the lid. She marks the level of the top of the dough with masking tape on the outside of the container and leaves it on the benchtop, at room temperature. Then she leaves for work.

   5.45 pm – When Paula returns, she checks on the bulk fermentation. The dough is a little under-fermented; it has risen but not quite by one-third of its original height, as it's winter and her house is cold. To catalyse further fermentation, she makes the oven steamy by putting a tray on the oven floor and filling it with boiling water. Then she places the container with the dough in the oven.

7 **6.45 pm – Final shape the dough.** Paula takes the container with the dough out of the oven. The dough has reached its one-third increase, so she shapes it ready for the tin.

For final-shaping instructions, see page 142.

8 **Transfer the dough.** Paula greases the tin with olive oil and puts the dough into it.

9 **6.50 pm – Proof the dough.** She tops up the tray on the oven floor with more boiling water, then puts the tin containing the dough in the oven and closes the door.

8.30 pm – Paula removes the tin containing the dough from the oven to finish proofing at room temperature. She turns the oven on to preheat to 250°C (475°F).

10 **9 pm – Bake the bread.** Paula does a poke test to see if the dough is properly proofed. It springs back slowly, so it's ready. She puts the tin containing the dough on a high shelf in the oven and closes the door.

For information about the poke test, see page 156.

9.30 pm – Paula checks on the bread. She slides the oven shelf holding the loaf towards her and knocks on the top of the loaf. It sounds almost hollow. She notices that one side is pale compared to the other side, so she turns the tin around, pushes the shelf back in, closes the oven door and gives it a further five minutes.

9.35 pm – Paula re-checks the bread. It's evenly golden now, but after knocking on the top of the loaf she's still unsure whether it's cooked. She grabs her food thermometer and sticks it into the loaf. Its internal temperature is 95°C (203°F). Yay! It's ready.

11 **Cool the bread.** Paula tips the loaf out of the tin onto a cooling rack and tries to wait for it to cool down. She manages 20 minutes and then must have a slice with a drizzle of olive oil; garlic rubbed across its hot surface; thinly sliced tomato; sprinkles of salt, pepper and oregano; and a few drops of chilli oil. Wonderful.

STEP 7

Divide the dough

In this step

Dough division requires a confident hand and quick, clean cuts. A plastic dough scraper or dough cutter makes dough cutting simple, and with gentle handling of the dough you will find even the wettest doughs easy to cut.

The purpose of cutting is to separate portions of dough from the mass. A mass of dough may represent two or many loaves. The goal is to cut the mass to produce equally sized doughs, so that every loaf cooks in the same timeframe.

How to divide

Put your kitchen scales on the benchtop. Tip the dough onto the benchtop and dust the top lightly with flour.

Now take a good look at the dough to discern how to divide it into the number of individual doughs you need. Dust your hands with a little flour. Then, using your dough scraper or cutter, begin to confidently cut away a portion of dough as close to the size you need as you can. Peel the dough portion away from the bulk and place it floured-side down on the scales. Repeat this until you have the number of portions you need, weighing them one at a time.

Getting equal portions

For your first bake with a particular weight of dough, you won't know what the weight of each dough portion needs to be until you've divided and weighed all your portions. If one portion turns out to be too heavy, cut some of it away and add it to the lighter doughs. If you're making several loaves of the same size, aim to get the portion weights within a range of about 20 g (0.7 oz).

This is what bakers do: they cut a bit of dough here and there to make sure all their dough portions are of equal weight, to ensure even baking.

Equal portion weights lead to even baking.

STEP 8
Preshape the dough

In this step

For more information

This step allows you to observe how well the gluten in your dough has developed and to test the effectiveness of your shaping technique. It's an important step only for free-form loaves,. With tin bread, the tin does all the holding of the loaf's shape, so you can skip this step and go straight to the final shaping.

For an experienced baker, preshaping can be as simple as rotating and tensioning dough to create a round shape, after which they move on to final shaping after a bench rest. But for beginners, preshaping is particularly important, because it gives you the opportunity to develop dough strength further, assess how well your dough holds its shape and to practise final shaping.

Don't be afraid to preshape more than once, to see whether your dough holds a boule (round) or bâtard (oval) shape successfully after a 15-minute rest. A lack of strength at this stage of the bread-making process can be assumed if there is a considerable loosening in the dough's shape after preshaping.

How to preshape dough

The first step is a simple preshape: a drag, rotate and tuck. To achieve this, place your right hand at the side of the dough closest to you to your right, and place your left hand at the side furthest from you to your left. Use both hands to simultaneously drag the dough across the benchtop surface towards you, rotate it anticlockwise and tuck its edges underneath.

For a beginner baker, I recommend letting the dough rest, covered, for 15 minutes, then rehearsing final-shaping steps for a boule (see page 144). After this rehearsal, you can move on to the bench rest and review.

Preshaping is an important step for free-form loaves.

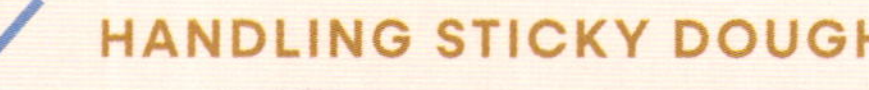

HANDLING STICKY DOUGH

The dividing, preshaping and final-shaping steps all benefit from confident, deft dough handling, something that can be difficult when you're a beginner baker. It can be tempting to handle the dough more and more, only to find it gets harder to work with, as it gets stickier. You might be tempted to add flour to get rid of its stickiness.

Instead, let the dough rest, covered, and give yourself a rest too. After 15 minutes, you will find the dough easier to handle. Don't hesitate to rest the dough multiple times to achieve the desired outcome. If, however, your dough is far, far too sticky and challenging to work with, then for your next bake, consider the following options:

- working with a different flour type
- using a lower hydration for the same recipe
- working with lower hydration recipes until you have more experience
- doing far more gluten development – that is, kneading.

Bench rest and review

As I said in the previous step, after preshaping or final-shaping rehearsal, leave the dough to rest, covered, on the benchtop. The amount of time given to bench resting can vary according to the number of loaves you have to preshape and, for home bakers, any demands that arise outside of bread baking.

For a commercial baker making perhaps 50 loaves, the bench rest lasts for the amount of time it takes to preshape all 50 doughs. For a home baker making only one or a few loaves, the bench rest can last from 15 to 30 minutes. Keep in mind that the dough continues to ferment during the bench rest. If it's a hot day, a short bench rest is best.

During the rest, the dough will either loosen a great deal or will hold its shape well. If the preshaped dough holds its shape well and doesn't flatten out considerably during the bench rest, you can confidently move to the final shaping. But if you return to the dough to find it has lost considerable height during the rest, then you'll need to preshape for a second time.

Preshaping twice or more

If the dough flattens out significantly during the bench rest, use a number of folding or kneading techniques (such as the lamination fold; see page 124) or repeat the final-shaping rehearsal to increase its strength. You are aiming for tighter folds and a tauter surface. Give the dough a 15-minute bench rest, covered, after every preshape or final-shaping rehearsal.

Do as many preshapes or final-shaping rehearsals and rests as you need for the dough to develop enough strength to hold its shape during the bench rest. Then move to the final shaping, knowing that your dough has the strength to hold that final shape.

I appreciate that terms like 'flatten out' are very subjective, but it isn't possible to give exact measurements for these steps. There are simply too many factors influencing dough performance to be able to make a single statement on how much flattening or loosening is acceptable. The preshape and bake will tell you best.

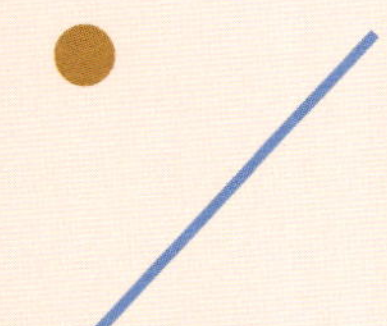

WHY IS THE DOUGH FLATTENING OUT?

If the dough flattens out a great deal during the bench rest, it's due to one of the following reasons:

- **The flour used wasn't a strong bread flour.**
- **The dough's hydration was too high, diluting the gluten strength.**
- **The gluten wasn't properly developed.**
- **The dough wasn't given enough time to rise by one-third during bulk fermentation.**
- **The shaping technique didn't create enough tension in the dough.**

STEP 9

Final shape the dough

The final shaping takes place just before you put the dough into a tin or proofing basket (banneton) for the final fermentation (proofing). The method for doing the final shaping differs from that for the preshaping, in that it creates a more defined shape (to suit how it will be baked – tin or free-form) and greater surface tension in the dough. The aim is to create a shape that the dough can hold during baking: you want both a tight coil in the dough and a taut outer skin.

The key to shaping is creating tension in the dough by folding it. The dough is always stretched with each fold (which further develops gluten). The number of folds is also important.

Tin loaves

For dough that will be baked in a tin, the final coil need not be too tight, because the tin's walls will support it. Looser shaping also allows tin breads to produce a slightly more open crumb. Make sure the coil is roughly the same size as the tin the dough will be baked in.

1. **Stretch the dough out a little on all sides to create a rectangle. Grab the two corners of the dough furthest from you and pull them to meet at the centre of the dough, as though you're making a paper plane, then push down on them to seal.**
2. **Take hold of the point you've created at the far side of the dough and start to roll up the dough towards you, creating a coil, until you've rolled one-third of the dough. Then with your fingers push down along the full width of the dough to seal the roll's edge to the flat part of the dough.**
3. **Start rolling again from the point at which you just made the seal, until you've rolled another third of the way towards you. Use your fingers again to seal along the width of the dough.**
4. **Roll up the final third.**
5. **Create tension in the dough by dragging the tube shape you have created across the benchtop.**

Create tension in the dough by folding it.

Free-form loaves

For free-form loaves, a taut coil is extremely important, because it's the only thing that will make the dough hold its shape. You want a dough that doesn't spread when it's tipped out of the proofing basket (banneton) just before baking.

There are a number of ways to shape a dough to create a boule (round) or a bâtard (oval) form. A particular shaping method can become popular and seem to be the best method of shaping and the one that will create the most open crumb, and yet you will see that bakers all over the world are creating open-crumb boules and bâtards with various shaping folds.

When it comes to very high hydration doughs, such as focaccia and pan de cristal, taut shaping cannot be achieved in the same way as it can in a boule or bâtard, and bakers don't expect to do so. Instead, they often rely on coil folds and no preshaping to bring this type of dough together, and they expect it to flatten out during bench rests and proofing.

To do the final shaping for a boule or bâtard, use the instructions given here as a starting point; as I've said, there are several ways to arrive at the correct shapes.

BOULE

1. Dust the dough surface lightly with flour, then flip the dough so that the floured side is on the benchtop.
2. Stretch the dough out a little on all sides to create a rectangle, then fold the right side of the dough into the centre, then fold the left side on top of the previous fold.
3. Grab the end closest to you, stretch it out, then fold it halfway across the two first folds.
4. Stretch the end furthest from you and bring it across towards you, to cover all the other folds.
5. Roll the dough towards you so the seams end up on the bottom of the dough.
6. Use the drag, rotate and tuck motion to tension the dough.

For drag, rotate and tuck instructions, see page 138.

1 — 2 — 3 — 4 — 5 — 6

BÂTARD

1. Follow the instructions on page 144 for a boule.
2. Press down on the boule and gently stretch out the dough – this gives you the space you need to fold the dough onto itself.
3. Fold the two top corners into the middle, overlapping, to create a triangular shape at the top.
4. Roll the top point of the dough into the middle and press down to seal.
5. Place your hands on either side of the dough and use your thumbs to press the dough into a tubular shape.
6. Continue to roll the dough towards you until you reach the end of the dough, then flip the dough over so the seam is facing up.
7. Grab the ends of the dough and fold them into the middle to neaten the tubular shape.
8. Finally, use your hands to gently roll the dough back and forth on the benchtop, causing it to elongate.

STEP 10

Transfer the dough

In this step

For more information

When you bake bread, you always have a choice: to make a tin loaf or a free-form loaf. Tin loaves are proofed in the tin, whereas free-form loaves are proofed in a proofing basket (banneton) and then transferred to a baking sheet, baking stone or flameproof casserole dish (Dutch oven) for baking.

Tin or free-form?

It's always easier to make bread baked in a tin than to make a free-form loaf, but there are several factors to consider when you're trying to decide – not least that free-form loaves are wonderful, and their challenges for a home baker are divine invitations to have great fun.

TINS

- Baking loaves in a tin is a great deal easier and contains fewer steps than baking free-form loaves.
- You can easily fit three loaves, and up to six loaves, of tin bread in a domestic oven.
- Most ovens will produce excellent tin loaves: tin bread can handle even low baking temperatures (as low as 190°C / 375°F) and still produce oven spring.
- Even a poorly developed dough, a dough made with low-gluten flour and a poorly shaped dough will rise and produce a loaf of bread with some height when baked in a tin.
- Tin bread is easier to slice and to make sandwiches with than free-form bread.

FREE-FORM

- You can create loaves of different shapes and signature loaves when you aren't constrained to the shape of a tin.
- The crumb in free-form loaves can be much more open than in tin loaves, if required.
- The home baker is often restricted to baking just one free-form loaf at a time. This is because most domestic ovens can only fit one flameproof casserole dish, and even if you don't use a casserole dish, boules and

Tin bread is easier to make, but proofing baskets give you more options for loaf shapes.

bâtards need to be baked on the top shelf of a home oven, where most of the steam produced by the tray of boiling water gathers.
- Free-form loaves absolutely must have temperatures very close to 250°C (475°F) if oven spring is to occur.

For more information about oven spring, see page 164.

Using a tin

A bread tin's sole purpose is to hold the shape of your dough and force it upwards when it rises, preventing it from spreading sideways, regardless of how poorly you have shaped it.

CARE AND USE

All bread tins benefit from being greased before the dough is placed in them. Any vegetable oil can be used. A pastry brush dipped into a small bowl of oil makes this an easy task; alternatively, you can use a spray bottle to create a thin coating.

Placing dough into a tin is extremely easy once you have gained some experience. At first you might create a lovely tube-shaped dough with a taut skin, then find yourself putting it sloppily in the tin, with the dough shape a little too wide.

A dough scraper dipped in water can be used on these occasions to neaten up the shape. Push the scraper down the tiny gap between the dough and tin on both sides to clean up any bits of dough clinging to the top of the tin's internal walls.

With practice, you'll better judge the width of the tin when shaping the dough and scoop the dough up deftly, landing it in the tin with a quick release.

Once the dough is in the tin, cover it to stop the surface from drying out. For this, you can use a plastic bag placed over the top or put the tin inside the bag (making sure the bag doesn't actually touch the dough); alternatively, use a very large metal bowl and invert it, or drape a wet tea towel over the tin. (The tea towel is my least favourite method, as it often sags and makes contact with the dough.)

To get the highest oven spring in a loaf of tin bread, always have water in a tray on the oven floor to create steam, and for a glossy finish, the moment you take the baked loaf out of the oven, spray its surface with water from a spray bottle.

Be sure to never wash a bread tin, unless you're using a silicone mould, as they can rust very easily. The tin is effectively cleaned every time it's used, because it's being sterilised in those high baking temperatures. If a tin must be washed because dough is getting stuck on its surface (a rare occurrence), be gentle, so as not to scratch its surface, then place it directly back in the oven to dry off quickly, as the oven will still be very warm after a bake.

Alternatively, turn the oven back on and bake off any dough stuck to the tin. After about 15 minutes at 250°C (475°F), it will easily break away when you take the tin out of the oven.

CHOOSING A TIN

Tin bread is so easy to bake that it matters little what type of tin you use as a home baker: all tins produce similar results. However, if you're going out to buy a new tin, the main two considerations with regards to bread baking are the material it's made from and the size of the loaf it will produce.

There are several materials to choose from, including aluminised steel, cast iron, glass, ceramic and silicone. Vessels made from metal are best, as they conduct heat far better than non-metal ones, allowing the bread to cook more quickly and a little more evenly than bread baked in a glass or ceramic bread pan.

The size of the tin matters. The size will directly affect how much dough you can bake in it and therefore the height of the final loaf. A baking tin with low sides will simply not hold as much dough as a taller tin, and the resulting loaf will be squat, not what we expect a loaf to look like; but it will be just as divine to devour.

Professional bread tins are a pleasure to use, because they are durable, strong and come in varying sizes, allowing you to choose exactly what size of loaf you want to bake. Loaves that come out of these tins look just like the loaves you would purchase from a gorgeous sourdough bakery.

Aluminised tins are so smooth that they rarely need to be oiled at all. They are made to last and are called 'professional' because they can be used over and over again by bakeries. The tins have dough capacity weights, helping bakers make informed decisions about the final loaf weight. Whichever tin you use, the most important factor is ensuring that you make a dough that is the right size for that tin.

For information about choosing the right tin size, see page 100.

Using a proofing basket

Proofing baskets (bannetons) can be oval or round, and they can be made from rattan, wood pulp waffle, plastic or hand-woven wicker. What they all have in common is a textured surface designed to trap flour to create a flour patina, which is important for preventing the dough from sticking to the basket.

For information about choosing the right proofing basket size, see page 100.

If you have purchased a new rattan, plastic or wood pulp basket, it's a good idea to season it. Lightly wet its entire surface with water by spraying it or by wiping it with a damp cloth. Sprinkle 4 tablespoons of rice flour or semolina inside the basket, then hold the basket on an angle and rotate it in your hands to allow flour to settle in all the grooves or waffles, until the entire surface has a coating of flour. Alternatively, you can dust the flour into the basket with a sieve. Rice flour or semolina are the flours for this task, as they are coarser than bread flour and less likely to be absorbed by the dough during proofing.

If you're using a wicker basket, line it with a cloth dusted in flour on the dough side,

rather than trying to give the basket a flour patina, as the spacings in the weave are a little too large.
All proofing baskets can be lined with a cotton cloth dusted in flour if you don't want the waffle or ridges to leave markings on your dough – for example, if you want to do intricate scoring. But most bakers really like the look of the basket patterns.

If you're doing an overnight proof in the fridge, lining your basket with a cloth and then giving the cloth a heavy dusting of flour are essential, as the long proofing time can result in the dough sticking to the basket. The wetter the dough, the heavier the dusting of flour should be.

If you don't have a proofing basket, there are numerous other kitchen vessels that can be used to support the dough – such as a small colander, soup bowl, fruit basket – so don't think you can't make a free-form loaf if you don't have a dedicated proofing basket. Line your vessel with a cloth heavily dusted in flour or with baking paper. Always give baking paper a good scrunch before lining the vessel, so that it softens and is more malleable and able to take on the shape of the dough. Place the dough into the vessel with its seams facing downwards and its smooth surface visible.

It is, of course, easier to remove a proofed dough from its shape-holding vessel – whatever that vessel may be – if the dough is sitting on baking paper, allowing you to simply lift the dough out on the paper. So why is this method not always used? The reason is that bakers like the textured pattern created on the surface of their dough by their proofing basket and choose to forgo ease in favour of aesthetics.

To place the dough in an unlined proofing basket, tip it in upside down, with the seams facing upwards and the smooth surface of the dough against the bottom of the basket. The side that is facing downwards now will become the top of the loaf when you tip the dough back out to bake.

After use, clean proofing baskets by using a dry brush to sweep out the excess flour. There is never a need to wash them or to use soap or dishwashing liquid. Soap will leave unwanted residue, fragrance and harmful chemicals in your basket. When it's time to bake your next loaf, flour the basket again and proceed.

STEP 11

Proof the dough

In this step

For more information

We're up to some of the final steps. The proofing is the second and final time the dough will be fermented.

Judging the rise

During the first (bulk) fermentation, you were waiting for the entire dough to rise by one-third of its original height. During the second fermentation, you want the dough to rise to 90% of its maximum rising potential. The final 10% will then be achieved in the oven, and is called 'oven spring'.

For more information about oven spring, see page 164.

You won't be able to measure the dough to know when it has reached 90% of its potential rise. Instead, you need to rely on lots of observation. Take photos of the dough and compare its early, middle and final proofing stages, so you can make informed judgements. Look at the dough frequently during proofing; it's the only way to see what's happening when you're learning.

You want the proofed dough to be full of bubbles, perhaps with a large bubble visible on the surface. It should be billowy, with a distinct rise.

To help you judge how much it has fermented and whether it has further to go, frequently do the poke test.

Poke the dough every 30 minutes to see differences in the fermenting dough. If you only poke it closer to the end of the proofing, you can't compare early pokes with later pokes. It will help you to decide what the dough springing back quickly looks like, compared to it springing back slowly. Observe and observe again. Keep the dough close to you, like a favourite family member or dear friend.

When the dough springs back slowly, it's properly proofed.

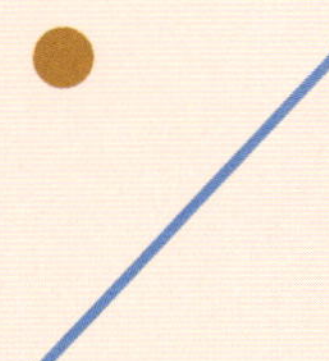

POKE TEST

As the dough rises in the tin or proofing basket (banneton), poke it firmly (but not hard) with a clean finger, then remove the finger immediately and watch what happens to the indent it made. There are three stages:

1. If the dough springs back quickly, completely filling the indent, it's underproofed. Give it more time.
2. If the dough springs back slowly, not completely filling the indent, it's properly proofed. Time to bake.
3. If the dough doesn't spring back, and the indent remains, it's overproofed. If it's overproofed there's nothing you can do: the bread is likely to flatten in the oven, and no oven spring will occur. However, the bread will still taste delicious.

It's important to put the dough into the oven to bake once it's properly proofed. This will ensure that oven spring occurs and you get an even rise and a crumb comprising a mixture of small and larger holes that are well distributed in an ordered pattern.

If you bake underproofed dough, instead of achieving a uniform rise of the entire dough, the dough will burst out at the top.

In contrast, if you bake overproofed dough, it will flatten out within minutes of hitting the oven.

If you feel unsure about where in the fermentation process your dough has reached, I recommend you err on the side of overproofing as opposed to underproofing. Even if it means a loaf flattens out during the bake, I prefer an overproofed crumb, which is uniform and well spread, to an underproofed crumb, which has a messy distribution of holes, distorted and odd looking.

Also, by allowing a dough to reach maximum proofing, you can make a note of this by taking a photo or by making a small mark on the tin or proofing basket (banneton) with a permanent pen. This will be useful when you make the same dough again and reach proofing stage once more. It will also be useful overall to see how the poke test performs in an overproofed dough, because only when you have seen what an overproofed dough looks like and how it responds to a poke test can you make sense of the proofing stages that come before it.

Controlling proofing speed

Many commercial bakeries use some kind of proofing chamber that lets them control the proofing speed by setting the temperature and humidity level. Proofing chambers ensure that proofing happens in a timely fashion regardless of changes in the ambient temperature and humidity.

As a home baker, you can control proofing speed by using your oven to speed things up or your fridge to slow things down, just as you can do for the bulk fermentation.

For more information about controlling fermentation speed, see page 132.

There are some additional considerations when it comes to slowing down the proofing using your fridge. This is because the dough is no longer in a clear container but in a tin or proofing basket (banneton), making it much more difficult to observe.

When you're starting out, I recommend that you do fridge proofing during the day, so that you can observe what's happening to your dough every few hours. As a beginner, don't do overnight proofing, as it means you can't assess the fermentation.

When you do a proof in the fridge, it's best to start the proofing at room temperature. Once you observe fermentation is occurring, with a slight rise of the dough, then you can put it in the fridge. Place the proofing basket or tin inside a plastic bag to prevent it from drying out. Remember to check your dough frequently.

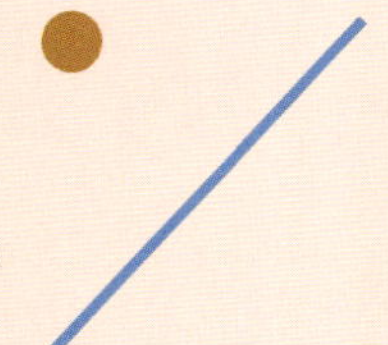

FREEZER PROOFING FOR SHAPE

If you fear that your dough is going to come out of the proofing basket (banneton) too loose, because you can see that it's clinging to the sides of the basket and that it won't hold its shape after it has completed proofing, put it in the freezer for 30 minutes before baking.

The cold temperature will stiffen the dough and reduce the amount of spread when you tip it out of the basket. It won't save the dough from some flattening out, but it may reduce the amount of flattening that occurs.

Preparing to bake

When proofing is complete, the next thing to do is prepare the dough to go into the oven.

If you completed the proof in a tin, you're ready to go: the dough will go into the oven in the same tin.

Alternatively, if your dough proofed in a proofing basket (banneton) or other shape-holding vessel, you need to transfer it from the vessel to a greased baking sheet or to an ungreased baking stone or flameproof casserole dish (Dutch oven).

If you lined the basket or vessel with baking paper before putting the dough into it, seam-side downwards, to proof, all you need to do is take hold of the sides of the baking paper and lift the dough to the baking sheet, stone or casserole dish. Some flameproof casserole dishes have a shallow skillet part, making this process safer and easier.

If you're using a dedicated proofing basket, you probably didn't line it with baking paper, because you want to see the lovely basket patterns on your bread. But if you're baking the dough in a flameproof casserole dish that doesn't come with a shallow skillet, I wouldn't recommend attempting to tip the dough straight into it, as it will be extremely hot.

Instead, put a piece of baking paper across the top of the proofing basket and sit a round plate upside down over it. Flip the plate and basket together to tip the dough onto the paper-lined plate. Place the plate onto the benchtop and lift off the basket to reveal the dough.

Score the dough using a lame (see overleaf), then lift the edges of the baking paper, balancing the dough on top, and lower the dough – still on the paper – into the flameproof casserole dish, being very careful not to touch the side of the dish with your hands. The dough can sit on the paper throughout baking.

STEP 11 – PROOF THE DOUGH

7 8 9 10 11 12 13

Scoring the dough

Scoring – cuts made to the top of bread doughs after proofing and just before baking – controls where the dough will open up and expand during baking. It can be used on tin loaves, but it's mostly used on free-form loaves, where it really shines.

If you don't score your dough, it will erupt in its weakest area, which may affect the aesthetic appearance of the final loaf. It won't change the flavour or nutritional qualities of the bread, the most important parts of bread making. But if you want to determine where the expansion happens, scoring is key.

Scoring is always done holding the knife or lame at an angle to the dough surface. The goal is to let the dough peel back from the cut to create an 'ear', and this won't be achieved with a cut made by a blade held perpendicular to the dough surface.

If you're working with an overproofed dough, scoring will be difficult, as the dough will be slack. Just aim for a single quick cut in the middle or the side of the loaf. Alternatively, place the dough in the freezer for 15–20 minutes to firm it up, and then scoring will be easier to do.

After scoring, especially if you make a single score along the length of the dough, the dough will begin to open up, and you should see the gluten matrix clearly on display. There will be lots of gluten strands crisscrossing just below the surface of the dough, indicating that excellent gluten development has occurred.

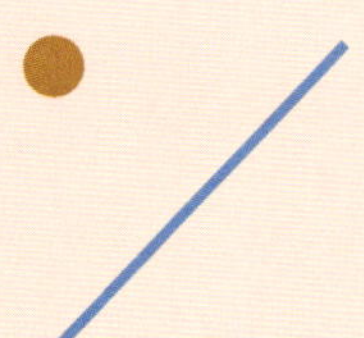

DETAILED SCORING

Scoring is used by some commercial bakers to create their signature look, to add artwork or to denote their different types of loaves. Scoring is easier when the dough is cold, so bakers who like to do detailed scoring will either start their proof outside the fridge and complete the proof inside the fridge, or will place the dough in the freezer for up to 30 minutes after the proof is complete. Both approaches create a very cold dough that is stiff, firm and easy to score.

STEP 12

Bake the bread

In this step

For more information

Oven temperatures

A high oven temperature is extremely important for making free-form loaves and pizzas. With free-form loaves, you need the oven to reach 250°C (475°F), or 230°C (450°F) at an absolute minimum. It needs to be much higher for pizza doughs. Without these high temperatures it can be hard to get excellent oven spring in a free-form loaf (it will flatten out a bit instead) and to adequately heat a flameproof casserole dish (Dutch oven) prior to placing the dough in it.

On the other hand, you can work with temperatures as low as 190°C (375°F) when you bake bread in a tin, because the dough can't flatten out; the tin walls prevent that.

Fruit breads, rye and enriched doughs, such as panettone, are full of extra wet ingredients or have very high hydrations, meaning they take longer to cook. But if the oven temperature is too high, the tops and sides of these loaves and any fruit on the surface will become charred. Set the oven to 250°C (475°F) to preheat it, then lower the temperature to 230°C (450°F) the moment you place the dough in the oven. After 20 minutes, reduce the temperature further, to as low as 180–190°C (350–375°F).

Preheating the oven

It's important that your oven is hot – 250°C (475°F) fan-forced – in time for your bake. This means turning it on before the proofing has finished, giving it enough time to reach the correct temperature. If your oven allows, have the temperature at 300°C (575°F). The oven temperature desired is, as I've said, 250°C (475°F), but home ovens are so small that the temperature drops significantly as soon as you open the

Happiness is when oven spring occurs.

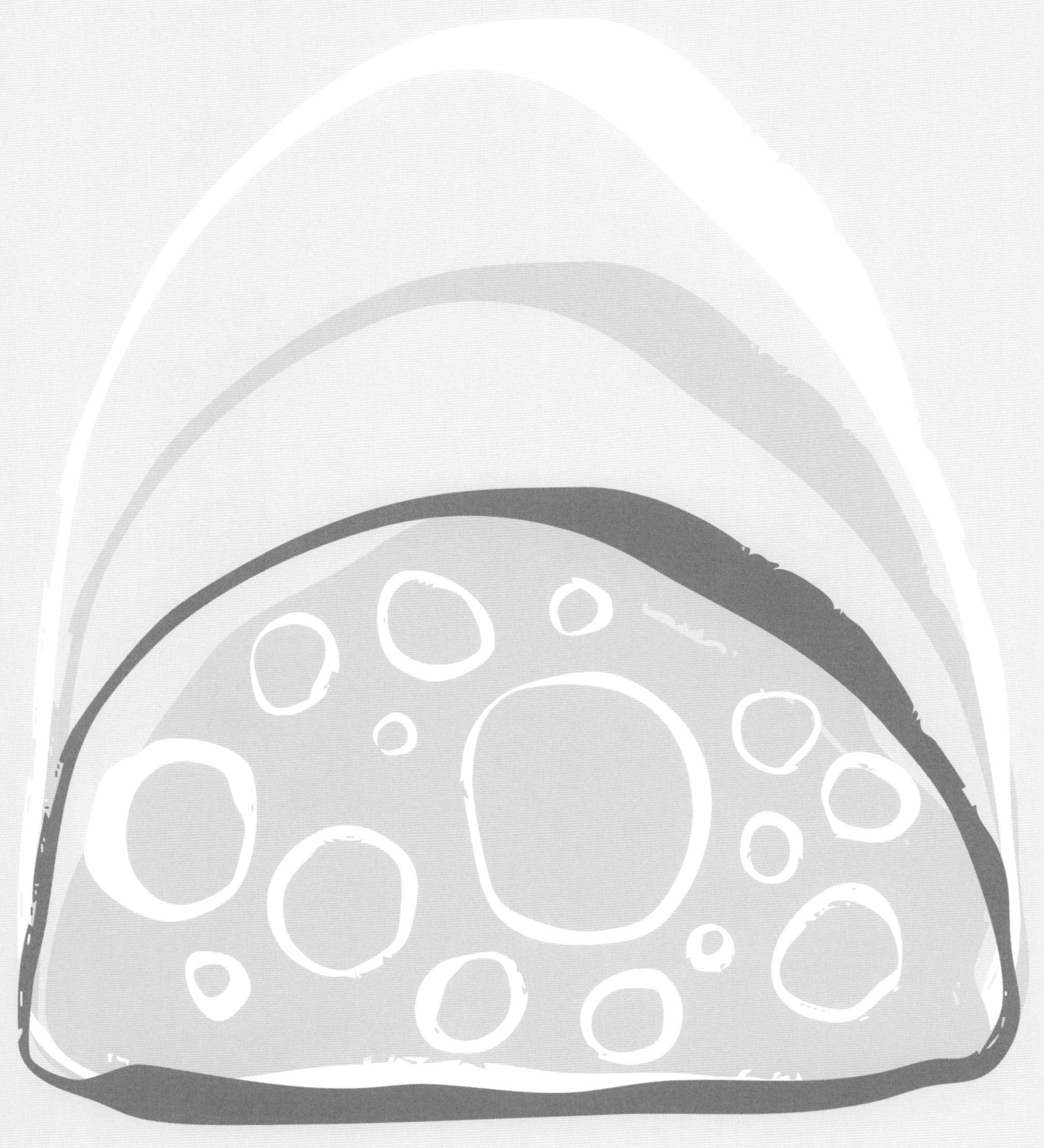

door. The moment you put the bread in the oven, lower the temperature to 250°C (475°F). If you have access to it, you can also use a higher temperature to heat your flameproof casserole dish.

I love being energy efficient – for many reasons, climate change being the biggest – so I turn my oven on with just enough time for it to come to temperature before baking. All ovens are different, so you'll need to work out how long before baking you need to turn on your own oven.

If you're not using a flameproof casserole dish for baking, before turning the oven on to preheat, place a large tray, or dish capable of holding liquid, on the oven floor. Bring the kettle to the boil, then carefully pour water from the kettle into the tray, making sure it doesn't overflow – about three-quarters full is enough. Then turn on the oven.

If you are using a flameproof casserole dish, you don't need the tray on the oven floor. Instead, before turning the oven on to preheat, put the casserole dish inside it, with the lid on ajar, then turn on the oven. Allow one hour to heat both the oven and the casserole dish.

Oven spring

Happiness is when oven spring occurs. This is a final burst of fermentation that causes your perfectly proofed dough to burst open as it rises to its maximum volume.

Having a steamy oven helps with oven spring. If you're not using a flameproof casserole dish to bake in, remember to place a tray containing water on the oven floor. You want a very humid environment for the first 20 minutes of baking, then a dry oven for the remaining baking time. As you gain experience, you'll be able to work out just how much water you need in the tray.

Baking times

At a high oven temperature of 250°C (475°F) fan-forced, most loaves take around 25–30 minutes to bake and to reach an internal temperature of 95°C (203°F). Variations in baking times can be caused by the size of the loaf and the flour and other ingredients used: wholegrain flour and fruit breads can take longer, because they hold on to moisture well. Your oven's personal characteristics, such as how well the door seals and how evenly the hot air is distributed in the oven chamber, may also affect baking times.

As every oven's heating effectiveness is different, check on your dough regularly by viewing it through the glass door. With the fan-forced function, the highest, steamiest point of the oven is best. If the top of your tin bread starts to look too dark too quickly (within about 15 minutes of going into the oven), you can turn the oven down to as low as 190°C (375°F) to finish the bake.

Have a spare, suitably sized baking tin to hand (avoid single-use aluminium foil if you can) and if the top of the dough is becoming too dark, place the spare tin, inverted, over the dough in the oven, to protect the surface. Remove the cover only once the bread is fully cooked.

If the bread still comes out too dark, next time you bake it, reduce the oven temperature from the initial 250°C (475°F) to 190°C (375°F) the moment you place the dough in the oven.

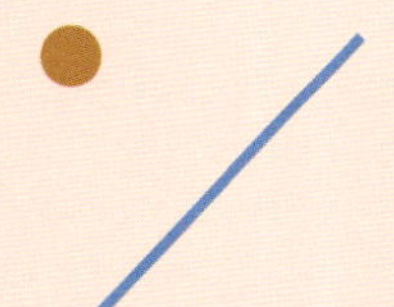

BAKING WITH A FLAMEPROOF CASSEROLE DISH

This is a clever way to ensure your dough gets the steam effect. The flameproof casserole dish (Dutch oven) creates a sealed environment that traps steam as moisture is released from the dough. It is used to bake free-form loaves, not tin loaves.

The casserole dish should be preheated inside the oven, so that you get the best steam effect right at the beginning of the bake. The dish needs to be extremely hot, no less than 250°C (475°F), to be truly effective.

Bake the dough for 20 minutes with the lid on the casserole dish, then for 10–15 minutes with the lid off.

STEP 13

Cool the bread

In this step

Finally, your loaf is ready. You'll be tempted to start slicing straightaway, and I appreciate why. With that wonderful aroma, who can resist?

Cooling basics

The moment a loaf is taken out of the oven, it needs to be cooled down to prevent a build-up of moisture at its base. Moisture will turn the bread soggy, undermine its crispiness and lead to an early onset of mould.

Cool tin loaves by tipping them out of the tin and placing them on a cooling rack. Remove free-form loaves from their baking sheet, baking stone or flameproof casserole dish (Dutch oven) and also place on a cooling rack. All parts of the loaf base should be raised from the benchtop surface. If you don't have a cooling rack, before heating your oven, remove one of its racks and use that.

If you want to keep the integrity of the bread crumb intact, it's important to let the loaf cool completely before slicing. When bread is warm, it's structurally weak. It will start to collapse the moment you put downward pressure on it with a knife.

It is also vital that you let the loaf cool completely before placing it in a plastic bag or food-storage container. As bread cools it releases a great deal of moisture, and if that moisture is trapped with it, it will take no time at all for mould to appear on the bread's surface.

Storing bread

My favourite way to store bread would be in an airtight, transparent, loaf-size container, to keep the inside moist and the crust crispy, but they are really hard to find. Most are not airtight or aren't transparent, and when you can't see the bread, even though the container is right there, the bread can be forgotten.

So, despite my contempt for plastic bags, I find myself resorting to them for bread storage. If you find a better solution, one that doesn't involve plastic and produces a truly airtight seal, brilliant.

Cut big, fat slices and slather them in butter and honey.

PART 4

Recipes

In this chapter you'll find recipes for some of my favourite breads and biscuits (cookies) that I regularly make with sourdough and discarded leaven (on the rare occasion that I produce discard). Not only do they celebrate the flexibility of sourdough and help to minimise waste, they will help you gain confidence when working with the Baker's Percentage. Below are my tips to help get your started.

WHOLEMEAL FLOURS AND LSA

The recipes in this chapter contain wholemeal leaven made with 100% hydration and use wholemeal (whole-wheat) flour. Some also include LSA (linseeds/flax seeds, sunflower seeds and almonds), which is rich in fibre. Although this will result in a less open crumb in your bread, I believe the benefits of this fibre-rich addition far outweigh the aesthetics of an open-crumb loaf.

'DISCARD' RECIPES

Some of the recipes use discard leaven, but remember it is possible to manage leaven so that discard is never produced. The exceptions are when you want to produce a bread with a very open crumb and a fast fermenting time (which requires feeding and discarding twice and up to three times a day), or if you are only baking once a month and have a very dry leaven and want to build fermenting speed into it.

MACHINE KNEADING

If you are using a stand mixer with a dough hook, start the knead on a slow setting to prevent the flour from flying out of the bowl. During the dough rests, cover the top of the machine bowl with plastic bags to stop the dough from drying out. This way you won't need to remove the dough hook – simply wrap the plastic bags around the top of the bowl on either side of the dough hook arm. All of the bread recipes can be made by using a stand mixer or by hand.

DOUGH TOO WET

If the dough feels too wet when you come to preshaping and final shaping your loaf, simply preshape it multiple times, combined with bench rests (see page 141), and it will firm up nicely.

BULK FERMENTATION

Straight-walled transparent food containers, whether rectangular or square, are excellent for observing bulk fermentation (I like to use Cambro food storage containers). Choose a container that allows the dough to touch all sides the moment you add the dough. This will prevent the dough flattening out and confusing you into thinking it has not risen much.

During bulk fermentation (see page 130), I recommend checking on your dough after two, three and four hours to observe how slowly or how quickly the dough ferments, depending on the ambient room temperature: look for a one-third rise, with a billowy and well-aerated dough. As you become more skilled, you can check on it less frequently.

PROOFING BASKET (BANNETON) AND TIN SIZE

Where relevant, the bread recipes in this book use a 680 g (1.5 lb) capacity tin and a 20 cm (8 in) internal diameter boule proofing basket (banneton).

CREATE A STEAMY ENVIRONMENT

Unless you are using a flameproof casserole dish (Dutch oven) to bake your bread, three-quarter fill a baking tray with water and place it on the oven floor to create a steamy environment. This will result in better oven spring. Each flameproof casserole dish has a maximum temperature potential; therefore, check the manufacturer's instructions.

CHECKING FOR DONENESS

To check that your bread is cooked all the way through, insert a food thermometer with a metal skewer into the centre of the bread. If the temperature reads 95°C (203°F), your bake is ready.

MAKE YOUR BREAD SHINE

If you'd like to make the top of your breads glisten, such as the honey buns on page 202, fill a spray bottle with water and lightly spray the surface of the bread the moment it comes out of the oven.

THE IMPORTANCE OF COOLING RACKS

With all bread recipes, it is important to place hot bread on a cooling rack the moment it comes out of the oven. If the bread is not elevated above the surface of your kitchen bench, there won't be adequate airflow and it will become moist and soft.

Everyday loaf

This is a lovely high-nutrition loaf to accompany daily meals. The long fermentolyse allows the wholemeal flour to become more pliable and easier to stretch. Enjoy with soups, as a breakfast toast or to make sandwiches.

- 467.5 g (16.5 oz) water (85% of flour weight)
- 110 g (3.88 oz) wholemeal (whole-wheat) leaven (20% of flour weight), made with 100% hydration
- 11 g (0.39 oz) salt (2% of flour weight)
- 275 g (9.7 oz) wholemeal (whole-wheat) flour
- 275 g (9.7 oz) white bread flour
- semolina or rice flour, for dusting

In a large bowl, add the water, leaven, salt and flours in this order. Mix very well with one hand until there are no dry flecks of flour remaining. Cover the bowl with a plate and leave to fermentolyse for 1 hour.

Knead the dough by completing 60 stretch and folds (see page 121). The dough will tear a little, but this is okay. Cover the dough and rest for 15 minutes, then complete a further 60 stretch and folds – the dough will tear far less this time.

Bulk ferment the dough by placing it in a lightly oiled transparent rectangular food container. Gently flatten the dough and mark its height on the container, then cover with a lid. Check the dough regularly, until it has risen by one-third (see page 130).

To preshape the dough, drag, rotate and tuck the dough to create a boule shape (see page 138). Cover the dough with an upturned bowl and rest for 15 minutes.

To complete the final shape, stretch out the dough and complete four folds (see page 144). Tension the dough surface using the drag, rotate and tuck technique (see page 138), then transfer the dough, seam-side up, to a proofing basket (banneton) with an internal diameter of 20 cm (8 in), dusted with semolina or rice flour (dust with extra flour if your baskets are new).

Cover the dough with an upturned bowl or a plastic bag to stop the surface from drying out, or place it on the top shelf of the oven, with a tray of boiling water on the oven floor to create a warm, steamy environment, and allow it to proof (see page 154). If you're proofing your dough in the oven, remove it before the proof has finished to give yourself time to preheat the oven.

Complete the proof at room temperature, covering the dough with an upturned bowl or plastic bag.

Top up the tray with more water or three-quarter fill a tray with water and place it on the oven floor, if you proofed the dough on your kitchen bench. Preheat the oven to 250°C (480°F) for 30–45 minutes.

Flip the dough onto a baking tray lined with baking paper and use a lame to score four cuts on an angle in a square shape on the top of the dough (see page 160). Transfer the dough to the oven and bake for 20–30 minutes, or until the internal temperature of the bread reaches 95°C (203°F) on a food thermometer. Turn out the loaf onto a cooling rack and leave to cool completely.

The loaf will keep stored in an airtight container or plastic bag for more than a week.

Village
Dreaming
Tomato
Jam

Rye loaf

This basic rye loaf recipe is even more delicious with the addition of caraway seed, a little honey (or other sweetener), dried fruit, such as cranberries, and nuts or seeds such as walnuts, sunflower seeds or linseed (flax seeds) (or a combination of all three). Feel free to increase or reduce the amounts I've suggested here, particularly the caraway seed, if it's not for you. Add these ingredients at the very beginning with the core ingredients.
This is a very sticky dough that develops only a small quantity of gluten from the white flour. Use a 450 g (1 lb) tin for this loaf.

- 522.5 g (18.4 oz) water (95% of flour weight)
- 110 g (3.88 oz) wholemeal (whole-wheat) leaven (20% of flour weight), made with 100% hydration
- 11 g (0.39 oz) salt (2% of flour weight)
- 385 g (13.6 oz) rye wholemeal flour, plus extra for dusting
- 165 g (5.82 oz) white bread flour

OPTIONAL ADDITIONS

- 5.5 g (0.19 oz) caraway seed
- 27.5 g (0.97 oz) crushed walnuts
- 27.5 g (0.97 oz) cranberries
- 50 g (1.76 oz) honey

In a large bowl, add the water, leaven, salt, flours and optional additions (if using) in this order. Mix very well with one hand until there are no dry flecks of flour remaining. Cover the bowl with a plate and leave to fermentolyse for 1 hour.

Working with rye flour is different from other flours, as you will not be able to stretch the dough until its third knead, when the white flour begins to add a little gluten (even then, the knead will be extremely limited). Keep the dough in the bowl and mix vigorously with one hand for 1 minute. Next, push the dough across the bottom of the bowl, squishing it from one side to the other for 1 minute. Essentially you are still stretching the dough, but instead of up and out of the bowl (stretch and fold) you are stretching it across the bowl's surface.

Alternatively, remove the dough from the bowl and repeatedly knead using your palm for 1 minute, pushing the dough as far away from you as you can and then back towards you. This will be messy and the dough will constantly tear, but this is exactly what should happen. Return the dough to the bowl.

Cover the bowl again and rest for 30 minutes, then repeat the kneading process.

After the second knead, transfer the dough to a lightly oiled transparent rectangular food container. Gently flatten the dough and mark its height on the container, then cover with a lid and leave to bulk ferment. Check the dough regularly, until it has risen by one-third (see page 130). Keep a close eye on the dough, as rye flour ferments vigorously once it gets going, especially if it's extremely fresh or freshly milled.

There's no need to preshape this dough, due to its low gluten content. Instead, lightly dust your kitchen bench with rye flour, then tip the dough onto it. Use your dough scraper to bring the dough together into a bâtard-like shape by dragging the dough across the kitchen bench with the support of the dough scraper. Unlike other doughs that involve folds, with this one we are just wanting to create a little bit of tension.

Use both hands to quickly and decisively lift the dough into the tin. Dust its surface generously with rye flour. This is done to create a rustic high-contrast aesthetic.

Cover the dough with a large, upturned bowl, plastic bag or tea towel and allow it to proof until it has almost doubled in height. We can't really use the poke test (see page 156) for this dough, as it will not spring back; instead look for a considerable change in height combined with lots of cracking in the flour and tiny pin-hole perforations in the dough.

Preheat the oven to 190°C (375°F). Three-quarter fill a baking tray with water and place it on the oven floor.

Transfer the dough to the oven and bake for 25–35 minutes, or until the internal temperature of the bread reaches 95°C (203°F) on a food thermometer. Turn out the loaf onto a cooling rack and leave to cool completely.

The loaf will keep stored in an airtight container for more than a week. If you live in a warm or humid climate, place the container in the fridge to prevent spoilage, as this bread is beautifully moist.

NOTE

To turn this loaf into a 100% rye loaf, replace the bread flour with the same amount of rye flour and increase the hydration to 130%.

Place the ingredients in a large bowl in the following order: leaven, salt, flour and optional ingredients (if using). Add 715 g (25.65 oz) of boiling water (this is a variation of the flour scald method) and quickly mix using a wooden spoon, until completely combined. Use a spatula to spoon the mixture into a well-oiled 450 g (1 lb) tin, then flatten the mixture with a wet spatula. Dust the surface generously with rye flour and allow to proof, covered, until the dough has almost doubled in size, with lots of cracking in the flour and tiny pin-hole perforations in the dough.

Follow the main recipe to bake the dough, then tip it out of the tin and allow to cool for 5 hours before slicing (this is due to the loaf's high moisture content and will make slicing easier).

Nut & seed loaf

This gorgeous nut and seed loaf is made deliciously fragrant with the addition of caraway and fennel seeds, which have a rich, vibrant flavour profile and also aid digestion. The walnuts add a lovely nutty texture, while the pumpkin seeds create a lush aesthetic in every slice.

- 360 g (12.7 oz) water (85% of flour weight)
- 135 g (4.76 oz) wholemeal (whole-wheat) leaven (30% of flour weight), made with 100% hydration
- 9 g (0.32 oz) salt (2% of flour weight)
- 250 g (8.81 oz) wholemeal (whole-wheat) flour
- 200 g (7 oz) white bread flour
- semolina or rice flour, for dusting

NUT & SEED MIX

- 40 g (1.41 oz) walnuts, chopped
- 55 g (1.94 oz) sunflower seeds
- 70 g (2.46 oz) pumpkin seeds (pepitas), chopped
- ¼ teaspoon caraway seeds
- ¼ teaspoon fennel seeds
- 20 g (0.7 oz) water

Before you start on the dough, combine the nuts and seeds in a bowl, then add the water and mix again. Cover the bowl with a plate and set aside.

In a large bowl, add the water, leaven, salt and flours in this order. Mix very well with one hand until there are no dry flecks of flour remaining. Cover the bowl with a plate and leave to fermentolyse for 1 hour.

Knead the dough by completing 60 stretch and folds (see page 121). Slowly add the nut and seed mixture while kneading, until completely incorporated.

Cover the dough and rest for 15 minutes, then complete a further 60 stretch and folds.

Bulk ferment the dough by placing it in a lightly oiled transparent rectangular food container. Gently flatten the dough and mark its height on the container, then cover with a lid. Check the dough regularly, until it has risen by one-third (see page 130).

To preshape the dough, drag, rotate and tuck the dough to create a boule shape (see page 138). Cover the dough with an upturned bowl and rest for 15 minutes.

To complete the final shape, stretch out the dough and complete four folds (see page 144). Any nuts and seeds sticking out of the dough can be pushed in so that they don't burn during baking. Tension the dough surface using drag, rotate and tuck technique (see page 138), then transfer the dough, seam-side up, to a proofing basket (banneton) with an internal diameter of 20 cm (8 in), dusted with semolina or rice flour (dust with extra flour if your baskets are new).

Cover the dough with an upturned bowl or a plastic bag to stop the surface from drying out, or place it on the top shelf of the oven, with a tray of boiling water on the oven floor to create a warm, steamy environment, and allow it to proof (see page 154). If you're proofing your dough in the oven, remove it before the proof has finished to give yourself time to preheat the oven. Complete the proof at room temperature, covering the dough with an upturned bowl or plastic bag.

Top up the tray with more water or three-quarter fill a tray with water and place it on the oven floor, if you proofed the dough on your kitchen bench. Preheat the oven to 250°C (480°F) for 30–45 minutes.

Flip the dough onto a baking tray lined with baking paper and use a lame to score four cuts on an angle in a square shape on the top of the dough (see page 160). You can also score a cross shape on the top of the dough, if you like. Transfer to the oven and bake for 25–35 minutes, or until the internal temperature of the bread reaches 95°C (203°F) on a food thermometer. Turn out the loaf onto a cooling rack and leave to cool completely.

The loaf will keep stored in an airtight container or plastic bag for more than a week.

Umami sesame seed & tahini loaf

With black and white sesame seeds, a dash of tamari soy sauce and a little tahini, this loaf has a wonderful light umami flavour. Feel free to ramp up the flavour with even more tahini and tamari. I love these flavours and I restrained myself with this recipe, just in case you prefer a mild-flavoured loaf. I love to serve it with soup.

- 440 g (15.5 oz) water (80% of flour weight)
- 110 g (3.88 oz) wholemeal (whole-wheat) leaven (20% of flour weight), made with 100% hydration
- 11 g (0.39 oz) salt (2% of flour weight)
- 150 g (5.3 oz) wholemeal (whole-wheat) flour
- 400 g (14.1 oz) white baker's flour
- 15 g (0.53 oz) white sesame seeds (2.72% of flour weight)
- 5 g (0.17 oz) black sesame seeds (0.9% of flour weight)
- 5 g (0.17 oz) tamari (0.9% of flour weight)
- 50 g (1.76 oz) hulled tahini (9.09% of flour weight)
- semolina or rice flour, for dusting

In a large bowl, add the water, leaven, salt, flours, sesame seeds, tamari and tahini in this order. Mix very well with one hand until there are no dry flecks of flour remaining. Cover the bowl with a plate and leave to fermentolyse for 30 minutes.

Knead the dough by completing 60 stretch and folds (see page 121). Cover the dough and rest for 15 minutes, then complete a further 60 stretch and folds. Cover and rest for 15 minutes.

Complete a final 60 stretch and folds, then transfer the dough to a lightly oiled transparent rectangular food container. Gently flatten the dough and mark its height on the container, then cover with a lid. Leave to bulk ferment, checking the dough regularly, until it has risen by one-third (see page 130).

To preshape the dough, drag, rotate and tuck the dough to create a boule shape (see page 138). Cover the dough with an upturned bowl and rest for 15 minutes.

To complete the final shape, stretch out the dough and complete four folds (see page 144). Tension the dough surface using the drag, rotate and tuck technique (see page 138), then transfer the dough, seam-side up, to a proofing basket (banneton) with an internal diameter of 20 cm (8 in), dusted with semolina or rice flour (dust with extra flour if your baskets are new).

Cover the dough with an upturned bowl or a plastic bag to stop the surface from drying out, or place it on the top shelf of the oven, with a tray of boiling water on the oven floor to create a warm, steamy environment, and allow it to proof

(see page 154). If you're proofing your dough in the oven, remove it before the proof has finished to give yourself time to preheat the oven. Complete the proof at room temperature, covering the dough with an upturned bowl or plastic bag.

Top up the tray with more water or three-quarter fill a tray with water and place it on the oven floor, if you proofed the dough on your kitchen bench. Preheat the oven to 250°C (480°F) for 30–45 minutes.

Flip the dough onto a baking tray lined with baking paper and use a lame to score four cuts on an angle in a square shape on the top of the dough (see page 160). Transfer to the oven and bake for 20–30 minutes, or until the internal temperature of the bread reaches 95°C (203°F) on a food thermometer. Turn out the loaf onto a cooling rack and leave to cool completely.

The loaf will keep stored in an airtight container for a week.

Fruit & bitter chocolate loaf

Fruit loaves are incredibly delicious, especially when toasted and slathered in butter. I love adding bitter chocolate to my fruit bread recipes – look for a brand that is not overly sweet, to make this bread truly shine.

- 360 g (12.7 oz) water (85% of flour weight)
- 135 g (4.76 oz) wholemeal (whole-wheat) leaven (30% of flour weight), made with 100% hydration
- 9 g (0.32 oz) salt (2% of flour weight)
- 250 g (8.81 oz) wholemeal (whole-wheat) flour
- 200 g (7 oz) white bread flour
- 20 g (0.7 oz) raw cacao powder or cocoa powder (4.5% of flour weight)
- semolina or rice flour, for dusting

Before you start on the dough, combine the fruit and chocolate mix ingredients except the alcohol in a large bowl (see ingredients on page 186). Add the Marsala or sherry, mix again, then cover with a plate and set aside.

In a large bowl, add the water, leaven, salt, flours and cacao in this order. Mix very well with one hand until there are no dry flecks of flour remaining. Cover the bowl with a plate and leave to fermentolyse for 1 hour.

Knead the dough by completing 60 stretch and folds (see page 121). Slowly add the fruit and chocolate mixture while kneading, until completely incorporated.

Cover the dough and rest for 15 minutes, then complete a further 60 stretch and folds.

Bulk ferment the dough by placing it in a lightly oiled transparent rectangular food container. Gently flatten the dough and mark its height on the container, then cover with a lid. Check the dough regularly, until it has risen by one-third (see page 130).

To preshape the dough, drag, rotate and tuck the dough to create a boule shape (see page 138). Cover the dough with an upturned bowl and rest for 15 minutes.

To complete the final shape, stretch out the dough and complete four folds (see page 144). Any fruit or chocolate sticking out of the dough can be pushed in so that it doesn't burn during baking. Tension the dough surface using drag, rotate and tuck technique (see page 138), then transfer the dough, seam-side up, to a proofing basket (banneton) with

FRUIT & CHOCOLATE MIX

40 g (1.41 oz) dates, pitted and finely chopped
90 g (3.17 oz) jumbo golden raisins (or any type of raisin or sultana)
25 g (0.88 oz) dried figs, dried fig rollup or candied figs (or any dried fruit of your choice), finely chopped
30 g (1.05 oz) walnuts, chopped
20 g (0.7 oz) berry jam (any kind)
5 g (0.17 oz) LSA
50 g (1.76 oz) bitter dark chocolate (at least 70% cocoa solids), roughly chopped
1 teaspoon ground cinnamon
⅛ teaspoon grated whole nutmeg (or ground nutmeg)
seeds from 1 green cardamom pod, finely crushed with a knife
80 g (2.82 oz) Marsala or sherry

an internal diameter of 20 cm (8 in), dusted with semolina or rice flour (dust with extra flour if your baskets are new).

Cover the dough with an upturned bowl or a plastic bag to stop the surface from drying out, or place it on the top shelf of the oven, with a tray of boiling water on the oven floor to create a warm, steamy environment, and allow it to proof (see page 154).

If you're proofing your dough in the oven, remove it before the proof has finished to give yourself time to preheat the oven. Complete the proof at room temperature, covering the dough with an upturned bowl or plastic bag.

Top up the tray with more water or three-quarter fill a tray with water and place it on the oven floor, if you proofed the dough on your kitchen bench. Preheat the oven to 250°C (480°F) for 30–45 minutes.

Flip the dough onto a baking tray lined with baking paper and use a lame to score four cuts on an angle in a square shape on the top of the dough (see page 160). Transfer to the oven and bake for 20 minutes.

Cover the top of the bread with an upturned baking tin to protect the top from overcooking, then reduce the oven temperature to 230°C (445°F) and continue to bake for a further 15–20 minutes, or until the internal temperature of the bread reaches 95°C (203°F) on a food thermometer. Turn out the loaf onto a cooling rack and leave to cool completely.

The loaf will keep stored in an airtight container or plastic bag for more than a week.

Herb-medley focaccia

Fresh herbs make everything taste fantastic, especially when combined with caramelised red onion and lightly fried garlic in this focaccia recipe. This is a very wet dough that is extremely extensible, so use a light touch when kneading and handling.

- 425 g (15 oz) water at 40°C (105°F) (85% of flour weight)
- 50 g (1.76 oz) wholemeal (whole-wheat) leaven (10% of flour weight), made with 100% hydration
- 10 g (0.35 oz) salt (2% of flour weight)
- 500 g (17.6 oz) white bread flour, plus extra for dusting

HERB, RED ONION & GARLIC FILLING

- 80 g (2.82 oz) olive oil
- 1 teaspoon salted butter
- 2 red onions, diced
- 80 g (2.82 oz) garlic, finely chopped
- 30 g (1.05 oz) mixed herbs, such as chives, thyme, rosemary and oregano, finely chopped
- 1 teaspoon fine salt

Line a 5 cm (2 in) deep, 32 cm x 22 cm (12½ in x 8¾ in) baking dish with baking paper.

To make the herb, red onion and garlic filling, heat the olive oil and butter in a large frying pan over low heat. Add the onion and cook, covered, for about 15 minutes, or until the onion is caramelised, sweet and very soft. Remove the lid and allow the onion to brown and crisp a little. Add the garlic and cook for 2 minutes, until lightly browned (don't overcook the garlic or its flavour will be lost), then remove the pan from the heat and set aside to cool.

In a large bowl, add the water, leaven, salt and flour in this order. Mix very well with one hand until there are no dry flecks of flour remaining. Cover the bowl with a plate and leave to fermentolyse for 30 minutes.

Using both hands, complete 20 coil folds (see page 123). Rest the dough for 15 minutes, then repeat the coil folds two more times with a 15-minute rest in between.

Using a quick, confident movement and the help of a dough scraper, lift the dough into a lightly oiled transparent rectangular food container and mark its height on the container. Cover with a lid.

Place a tray on the oven floor and add enough boiling water to come halfway up the sides of the tray. Place the container on the highest rack, then close the door and allow the dough to bulk ferment until it has risen by one-third (see page 130), checking at the 2-hour mark to make sure it has not risen too much, and adding more boiling water to the tray to speed up fermentation, if necessary.

Lightly spray your kitchen bench with a thin film of water. Gently tip the dough onto the damp bench, using a dough scraper to help remove the dough from the container.

Use your fingers to stretch out the dough. Grab a small amount of dough at one edge and pull it out deftly and gently – with a dough like this it's all about light, quick fingertip movements. Stretch the dough out from all sides as far as it will go – it should easily stretch to a 50 cm x 40 cm (19½ in x 15¾ in) rectangle. If the dough starts to tear, rest it for 15 minutes before continuing.

Continue to stretch the dough out a little more – it should be three to four times larger than when you first tipped it out.

Scatter one-third of the mixed herbs over the dough, followed by half the onion mixture. Working from left to right, roll up the dough until you reach the end. You will now have a long cylinder of dough with the length running perpendicular to the kitchen bench. Scatter the dough with another one-third of the herbs and the remaining onion mixture. Grab the top of the dough and fold it down to the middle of the dough, then grab the bottom and fold it up and away from you to completely cover the previous fold. Rotate the dough so that it is seam-side down, then complete three coil folds (see page 123). Transfer the dough to the prepared baking dish, then use your fingers to gently push the dough out until it almost fills the dish.

Transfer the baking dish to the top shelf in the oven, add more boiling water to the baking tray and allow the dough to proof until you see a billowy surface.

Remove the baking dish from the oven and cover with a plastic bag to help trap moisture. Continue to proof, at room temperature, for 1 hour or until the dough has risen slightly and is even more billowy. Sprinkle the remaining herb mixture and the salt over the dough.

Meanwhile, preheat the oven to 250°C (480°F). Leave the water-filled tray inside the oven.

Bake the focaccia for about 20 minutes, until the base is dry and an internal temperature of 95°C (203°F) is reached on a food thermometer.

Allow the focaccia to cool slightly, then cut into slices and enjoy. Any leftover focaccia will keep in an airtight container for a week, but it's so delicious I am sure it will be eaten within a day.

Spelt pizza dough

This recipe makes enough for one large pizza; simply double or triple the recipe to make more. As this dough contains buckwheat and wholemeal spelt flour, it won't have an open crumb but instead will be packed with flavour.

- 161 g (5.68 oz) water (70% of flour weight)
- 46 g (1.62 oz) wholemeal (whole-wheat) leaven (20% of flour weight), made with 100% hydration
- 5 g (0.17 oz) salt (2% of flour weight)
- 120 g (4.23 oz) wholemeal (whole-wheat) spelt flour
- 90 g (3.17 oz) white bread flour, plus extra for dusting
- 20 g (0.7 oz) buckwheat flour
- ½ teaspoon LSA

In a large bowl, add the water, leaven, salt, flours and LSA in this order. Mix very well with one hand until there are no dry flecks of flour remaining – the mixture will be sticky due to the high proportion of wholemeal flour. Cover the bowl with a plate and leave to fermentolyse for 30 minutes.

Knead the dough by hand – due to the stickiness of the dough, use the slap and fold kneading technique (see page 122). Complete 30 slap and folds, then cover the dough again and rest for 15 minutes. Repeat this process two more times with a 15-minute rest in between.

Bulk ferment the dough by placing it in a lightly oiled transparent rectangular food container. Gently flatten the dough and mark its height on the container, then cover with a lid. Check the dough regularly, until it has risen by one-third (see page 130). As there is only a small quantity of dough, the change in height will be modest, so you'll need to watch it closely.

To preshape the dough, drag, rotate and tuck the dough to create a boule shape (see page 138). Cover the dough with an upturned bowl and rest for 15 minutes.

Transfer the dough to a large well-oiled pizza tray or a square or round baking tray. Use your fingers to begin to stretch the dough out a little, then dust the top of the dough lightly with bread flour and push the palm of your hand into the middle of the dough to further stretch it out, working across the entire dough surface. Continue using your fingers and palm to push the dough into a square or round pizza base, about 5 mm (¼ in) thick. Leave the edges a bit thicker if you like a chunkier crust.

NOTE

Unfortunately, home ovens don't reach the hot temperatures achieved by commercial pizza ovens, which can reach temperatures between 350°C (660°F) and 400°C (750°F), to produce really crispy air-filled and slightly charred pizza edges.

Cover the dough and leave to proof at room temperature, until you see a little loftiness in the dough or a bubble or two. Preheat the oven to 250°C (480°F) or as high as your oven will go (see Note). If you have a pizza stone, then preheat this too; the thermal mass of the stone will hasten the cooking of your pizza.

Transfer the dough to the pizza stone (if using) or place the tray in the oven and bake for 5–10 minutes (depending on the heat of your oven), until the base of the dough starts to feel dry. Add your chosen toppings during the last few minutes of cooking, just enough to warm them through and melt the cheese. (I like to precook my toppings and add them when the pizza base is almost cooked, with a minute or so remaining. This way the toppings retain their colour and don't overcook.

Baguettes

This recipe makes three baguettes. The addition of wholemeal flour adds a lovely nutty flavour to these gorgeous breads.

- 262.5 g (9.26 oz) water (70% of flour weight)
- 75 g (2.64 oz) wholemeal (whole-wheat) leaven (20% of flour weight), made with 100% hydration
- 7.5 g (0.26 oz) salt (2% of flour weight)
- 125 g (4.4 oz) wholemeal (whole-wheat) spelt flour
- 250 g (8.82 oz) white bread flour, plus extra for dusting

In a large bowl, add the water, leaven, salt and flours in this order. Mix very well with one hand until there are no dry flecks of flour remaining. Cover the bowl with a plate and leave to fermentolyse for 30 minutes.

Knead the dough by completing 60 stretch and folds (see page 121). Cover the dough and rest for 15 minutes, then complete a further 60 stretch and folds.

Bulk ferment the dough by placing it in a lightly oiled transparent rectangular food container. Gently flatten the dough and mark its height on the container, then cover with a lid. Check the dough regularly, until it has risen by one-third (see page 130).

Tip the dough onto a lightly floured kitchen bench. Divide the dough into three equal pieces and shape each piece into a rectangle.

NOTE
If you love making baguettes, look for a dedicated baguette oven tray for even better results.

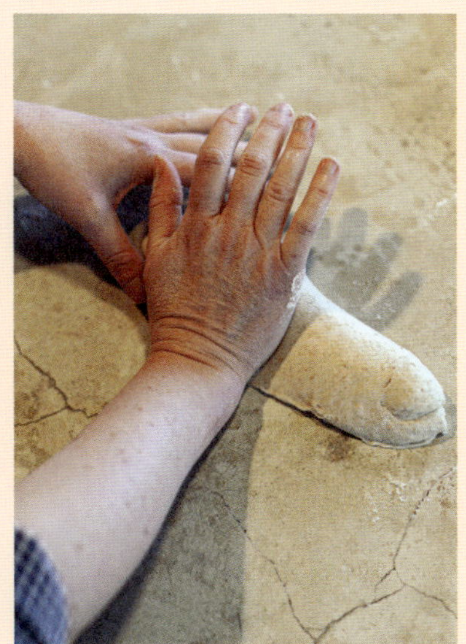

Working with one piece at a time, preshape the dough.

Use the palm of your hand to firmly flatten the dough into a 15 cm x 10 cm (6 in x 4 in) rectangle, with a long edge facing you. Simultaneously fold the left and right sides of the dough into the middle so they meet, and press down firmly on the folds. You should now have a smaller rectangle with its length running perpendicular to the kitchen bench. Grab the top of the dough and fold it one-third of the way down and press to seal, then repeat with the bottom edge to create a cylinder. Roll the dough over, so the seam side is facing down. Repeat these steps with the remaining pieces of dough, then cover with an upturned bowl and rest for 15 minutes.

To complete the final shape, flip a cylinder of dough so that the seam is facing up. With the long edge facing you, gently pat the dough to flatten it back into a small rectangle. Now we will do buisness letter folds. Grab the top of the dough and fold it two-thirds of the way down and press down firmly to seal. Be sure to maintain a rectangular shape the entire time you handle the dough.

Rotate the dough 180 degrees, so that the folded edge is closest to you, then grab the top of the dough again and fold it two-thirds of the way down and press down firmly to seal. You should now have a long flat cylinder, with its length running parallel to the kitchen bench. Starting at the right-hand end of the cylinder, fold the top of the dough into the middle, using the heel of your other hand to press down on the dough to seal it. Continue to work your way across the length of the dough, then roll the dough over, so that the seam side is facing down.

To elongate the dough into a baguette shape, place the palm of your dominant hand in the middle of the dough cylinder and roll it back and forth while pressing down to make the dough long enough for both your palms to continue the roll. With both hands and outstretched fingers, roll the cylinder back and forth from the middle towards the ends, until the dough is about 35 cm (14 in) long. Taper the baguette ends by pressing a little more firmly towards the end of the dough while rolling it back and forth. The baguette's final shape is complete. Repeat with the remaining dough.

Line a large baking tray with three sheets of baking paper, ensuring there is a large overlap between each sheet and that the paper overlaps the sides of the tray. Place the first baguette on the right side of the tray, then fold the baking paper on the left side of the baguette up into a small pleat. The pleat helps separate each baguette and stops them sticking together. Place the next two baguettes on the tray, making another pleat between each one. To further ensure the baguettes don't spread, place one or two ovenproof rolling pins to the left of the third baguette.

Transfer the baguettes to the oven, place a tray of boiling water on the oven floor to create a warm, steamy environment, and allow the baguettes to proof. Observe the solid form of the baguettes prior to the proof, then as they proof look at how they become bloated with air. Before they finish proofing, remove the tray with the baguettes from the oven and complete the proof at room temperature to allow time for preheating the oven.

Preheat the oven to 250°C (482°F) and top up the tray with more water, if necessary.

Just before transferring the baguettes to the oven, score them with a lame. Visualise a line in the middle of each baguette. You are looking to make three cuts along the length of this imaginary line in thirds. The first cut is done from the top of the baguette to about one-third of the way down. Add a second cut, overlapping the end of the first cut by 3 cm (1¼ in), and running parallel to it. Repeat to make a third cut to the bottom of the baguettes. These overlaps give the baguettes their signature look. Remove the rolling pins and place the tray with the baguettes in the oven.

Bake the baguettes for 20–25 minutes, until they reach an internal temperature of 95°C (203°F) on a food thermometer and look golden brown.

Turn out the baguettes onto a cooling rack and leave to cool completely.

Cornbread

Cornbread is extremely easy to make and is a wonderful alternative to wheat-only breads. I often use polenta to make hearty Italian porridge-like meals, accompanied with a rich lentil sauce; hence, I always have a supply of polenta in my pantry.

SERVES 8

- 500 g (17.6 oz) polenta
- 325 g (11.5 oz) water
- 30 g (1.06 oz) salted butter, finely chopped
- 80 g (2.82 oz) wholemeal (whole-wheat) flour
- 200 g (7 oz) wholemeal (whole-wheat) leaven discard, made with 100% hydration
- 250 g (8.82 oz) sweetcorn kernels, from 2 corn cobs (or use tinned)
- 16 g (0.56 oz) salt
- 300 g (10.6 oz) mild-flavoured olive oil, plus 2 tablespoons extra
- 60 g (2.12 oz) honey
- 3 eggs, beaten
- 1 red onion, finely chopped

Line a 5 cm (2 in) deep, 40 cm x 24 cm (15¾ in x 9½ in) baking tray with baking paper. Don't worry if you don't have a tray that's exactly the right size – anything with a bit of depth will work.

Place the polenta flour in a large mixing bowl. Bring the water and butter to the boil in a small saucepan, then pour over the polenta flour and mix well. Add the wholemeal flour, leaven discard, sweetcorn, salt, the 300 g (10.6 oz) olive oil, honey and eggs and mix very well with a wooden spoon until combined. Pour the cornbread mixture into the prepared baking tray and rest for 2 hours – this enables the leaven to start fermenting the flours, resulting in a loftier cornbread.

Preheat the oven to 220°C (430°F).

Transfer the tray to the oven and bake for 35–40 minutes, or until the cornbread is golden brown and a skewer inserted into the centre comes out clean.

Meanwhile, heat the remaining 2 tablespoons olive oil in a large frying pan over low heat, add the onion and cook, covered, for about 15 minutes, or until the onion is caramelised, sweet and very soft.

Serve the cornbread warm, topped with the caramelised red onion, with a hearty stew or soup or as an afternoon snack.

The cornbread will keep in an airtight container in the fridge for up to a week.

Honey buns

These honey buns are lovely! I use a high leaven percentage in this recipe simply because I want to speed up fermentation when using a weak leaven. I decreased the water hydration to compensate for the high amount of leaven and honey. The honey in this recipe complements the acidity of the leaven. I like to use these buns for mini hamburgers.

MAKES 6–7

- 260 g (9.17 oz) water (65% of flour weight)
- 160 g (5.64 oz) wholemeal (wholewheat) leaven (40% of flour weight), made with 100% hydration
- 8 g (0.28 oz) salt (2% of flour weight)
- 1 tablespoon honey
- 270 g (9.52 oz) wholemeal (wholewheat) spelt flour
- 130 g (4.58 oz) white bread flour, plus extra for dusting

In a bowl, add the water, leaven, salt, honey and flours in this order. Mix very well with one hand until there are no dry flecks of flour remaining. Cover the bowl with a plate and leave to fermentolyse for 30 minutes.

Knead the dough by completing 30 stretch and folds (see page 121). Cover the dough and rest for 15 minutes, then complete a further 30 stretch and folds.

Bulk ferment the dough by placing it in a lightly oiled transparent rectangular food container. Gently flatten the dough and mark its height on the container, then cover with a lid. Check the dough regularly, until it has risen by one-third (see page 130).

Tip the dough out onto a lightly floured kitchen bench and divide it into 6–7 pieces.

You don't need to preshape the dough balls as they are small and hold their shape well. To form the buns, take a piece of dough, then fold the edges into the middle and press down to seal. Flip the dough so the seam is underneath, then, using one hand, drag the dough in a tight circular movement to create a mini boule (bun). Repeat with the remaining pieces of dough.

Transfer the buns to a baking tray lined with baking paper, then cover with an upturned tray and proof at room temperature for about 1 hour, until they have increased in size and are billowy.

Meanwhile, preheat the oven to 250°C (480°F).

Remove the upturned tray, transfer the buns to the oven and bake for about 15 minutes, until golden brown. Turn out the buns onto a cooling rack and leave to cool.

Place in an airtight container and enjoy within 3 days.

Parmesan & fennel seed crackers

I love the rich flavour imparted by the freshly grated parmesan, rosemary and fennel seeds in these crackers. Be sure not to overcook them; otherwise, their texture will be compromised.

- 40 g (1.41 oz) rosemary leaves, finely chopped
- 1 teaspoon salt
- ½ teaspoon freshly ground black pepper
- 115 g (4 oz) plain (all-purpose) flour, plus extra for dusting
- 115 g (4 oz) wholemeal (whole-wheat) flour
- 50 g (1.76 oz) olive oil
- 100 g (3.52 oz) wholemeal (whole-wheat) leaven discard, made with 100% hydration
- 60 g (2.12 oz) water
- ½ teaspoon fennel seeds
- ⅓ cup finely grated parmesan

Preheat the oven to 190°C (375°F). Line a baking tray with baking paper.

Combine the rosemary leaves, salt and black pepper in a small bowl.

Place the flours, olive oil, leaven discard, water, fennel seeds, three-quarters of the rosemary mixture and the parmesan in a large bowl and mix to combine. Knead for about 2 minutes, until you have a firm dough, then cover and set aside to rest for 30 minutes.

Lightly dust your kitchen bench with flour, then roll out the dough until it is about 2 mm (⅛ in) thick. Carefully transfer the dough to the prepared tray and sprinkle with the remaining rosemary mixture. Use a knife to gently score the dough along its shortest length – this will make it easier to separate the dough into individual crackers once they're cooked.

Transfer the tray to the oven and bake for 20–30 minutes, or until the cracker sheet is lightly golden.

Allow the cracker sheet to cool, then test for crispness. If they're not crisp, continue to bake for a further 5–10 minutes, then cool again. Break the cracker sheet into shards or different-shaped pieces.

The crackers will keep in an airtight container for months, but you will have eaten them before then. Enjoy with dips of all kinds or with quince paste and Shropshire cheese – I love strong flavours!

Dill seed & red onion mini flatbreads

These mini flatbreads are delicious on their own as a mid-morning snack, or to accompany a curry, served with a dollop of yoghurt, a sprinkle of chilli and a bowl of warm rice.

MAKES 6–8

- 50 g (1.76 oz) wholemeal (whole-wheat) flour
- 30 g (1.05 oz) white bread flour
- 70 g (2.47 oz) wholemeal (whole-wheat) leaven discard, made with 100% hydration
- 1 tablespoon olive oil, plus extra for brushing
- 1 tablespoon water
- ½ teaspoon dill seed
- 30 g (1.05 oz) finely sliced red onion
- ½ teaspoon LSA
- 30 g (1.05 oz) grated cheddar
- 1 garlic clove
- chopped mixed herbs, to serve (optional)

Place all the ingredients except the garlic clove and herbs in a bowl and mix extremely well to form a rough dough. Knead the dough inside the bowl for 1 minute – we are not trying to develop gluten, the dough simply needs to be cohesive – then cover with a plate and rest for 1 hour at room temperature.

Divide the dough into golf ball-sized balls, then use your palms to gently flatten the dough into 1 cm (½ in) thick rounds.

Heat a frying pan over medium heat and brush with a little olive oil. Working in batches, cook the flatbreads for about 2 minutes each side, until cooked through and golden, reducing the heat slightly if they're browning too quickly. Brush the frying pan with additional oil after each batch.

Transfer the cooked flatbreads to a chopping board, brush each side with olive oil and rub with the garlic clove. Finish with a sprinkling of chopped mixed herbs, if you like.

Serve warm.

Sultana & lavender biscuits

I grow lots of lavender at ORTO Farm and distil it to make essential oil, which we use in our soap-making classes. I also add lavender to drinks, such as hot chocolate and herbal tea infusions, and in these scrumptious biscuits.

MAKES 6–8

- 330 g (11.64 oz) plain (all-purpose) flour
- 60 g (2.12 oz) milk
- 250 g (8.82 oz) wholemeal (whole-wheat) leaven discard, made with 100% hydration
- 60 g (2.12 oz) cold butter, finely diced
- 45 g (1.59 oz) white sugar
- ¼ teaspoon fine salt
- 2 small eggs, well beaten
- 1 teaspoon LSA
- 200 g (7 oz) sultanas (golden raisins)
- ½ teaspoon crushed lavender seed
- 100 g (3.52 oz) rolled (porridge) oats
- 50 g (1.76 oz) bitter dark chocolate (70% cocoa solids), roughly chopped

Preheat the oven to 180°C (350°F). Line a baking tray with baking paper.

Use a stand mixer with the paddle attached to mix the flour, milk, leaven, butter, sugar, salt and egg until smooth. Remove the bowl from the stand mixer and add the LSA, sultanas, lavender and rolled oats. Mix with a wooden spoon until very well combined. Break off pieces of dough and roll into 6–8 balls just a little larger than a golf ball. Gently flatten each piece of dough with your palm, then transfer to the prepared tray.

Bake the biscuits for 25–35 minutes, or until golden brown. For extra deliciousness, place a small piece of bitter dark chocolate on top of each biscuit a few minutes prior to removing the biscuits from the oven.

The biscuits will keep in an airtight container for up to 3 weeks.

Summer bounty pudding cake

We produce lots of berries on our property, ORTO Farm, from strawberries to currants, blueberries and boysenberries. I turn these berries into compotes and preserves and use them to make desserts in winter. This pudding-like cake is a favourite because it allows me to use my fruit bounty.

SERVES 6

- 150 g (5.3 oz) salted butter, softened
- 40 g (1.41 oz) very mild-flavoured olive oil
- 160 g (5.64 oz) honey (add an extra 40 g / 1.41 oz if you like your desserts very sweet)
- 100 g (3.52 oz) wholemeal (whole-wheat) leaven discard, made with 100% hydration
- 150 g (5.3 oz) plain (all-purpose) white flour
- 50 g (1.76 oz) very fine polenta
- 2 teaspoons baking powder
- pinch of salt
- 2 large eggs
- 30 g (1.05 oz) milk
- 50 g (1.76 oz) nut meal of your choice (I like to grind pumpkin seeds/pepitas, walnuts and shelled pistachios very finely)
- 550 g (19.4 oz) minimal-sugar boysenberry fruit compote (or any fruit compote you like)

HONEY SYRUP TOPPING

- 40 g (1.41 oz) salted butter
- 50 g (1.76 oz) honey
- 2 teaspoons ground cinnamon
- 2 eggs

Line a 10 cm (4 in) deep, 22 cm (8¾ in) round baking dish with baking paper.

Using a stand mixer with the paddle attached, beat the butter, oil and honey until the butter is creamed. Add the leaven discard and mix well until fully incorporated.

Sift the flour, polenta, baking powder and salt into a separate bowl and mix well. Add the flour mixture to the creamed butter mixture and use the stand mixer to mix until fully combined, with no flecks of dry flour remaining.

Lightly whisk the eggs and milk in a bowl. Add the egg mixture to the batter and mix until well combined. Pour the batter into the prepared dish and smooth the top. Sprinkle the surface with the nut meal and spread the berry compote over the top. As the pudding cooks, the compote will seep into the batter layer underneath.

Preheat the oven to 190°C (375°F).

To make the honey syrup topping, melt the butter in a small saucepan over low heat. Add the honey and cinnamon and stir to combine. Remove the pan from the heat and set aside to cool. Whisk the eggs in a small bowl, then add to the cooled honey syrup and stir through to combine.

Transfer the pudding to the oven and bake for 30 minutes. Remove the dish from the oven and pour the syrup over the top, then return to the oven and continue to bake for 20 minutes, or until a skewer inserted into the pudding comes out clean.

Enjoy with yoghurt, cream or warm milk.

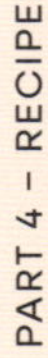

Panettone ti amo (Panettone, I love you)

I make this delicious celebration bread almost every Christmas. At first, I started making panettone in a tin, as it was an easy way to make this gorgeous project happen during a very busy season. Over the years I started to order traditional panettone moulds and that's when the fun really started. I have hits and misses with making it, simply because it requires such concentrated dedication, including making a new milk leaven and one that is super strong and able to complete its fermentation in 3–4 hours. When I have a hit, it comes out so very deliciously perfect, truly light and with a fantastic crumb. When I have less of a hit, it comes out heavy, but still full of flavour, especially when dipped in a *caffe latte*, or toasted with lashings of butter. When I have a hit my daughters say, 'Mum, it tastes just like the real one!', and I say, 'surely, it's even better!'. I most definitely think so. *Buon natale a tutti!*

A stand mixer or a friend is required for this recipe
This recipe requires a great deal of kneading and a stand mixer with a dough hook is highly recommended. Alternatively, invite a friend or two over and celebrate the lead up to the end of the year with a weekend of panettone making and kneading; it is absolutely one of my favourite ways to spend time together.

Warm temperatures are really important for making panettone
When it comes to making any enriched bread that contains milk and fats, temperature is crucial to creating an effective fermentation speed, because without warmth these recipes take far too long to make. So, use your oven for all parts of this recipe, with steaming hot water in its base, to support fermentation speed, including the milk leaven fermentations.

Ingredients and the Baker's Percentage
In an enriched bread like this one, when it comes to hydration, the Baker's Percentage can appear completely wrong. Where is the water component? There is no water. However, water is present in the milk, eggs and butter.

Traditional panettone baking paper moulds and metal skewers
The final proof and baking of panettone take place in a patterned and rigid paper panettone mould, which is readily available online. The mould size for this recipe is 11 cm (4½ in)

high and 16 cm (6½ in) in diameter. You will need to insert two metal skewers 3 cm (1¼ in) above the base of the mould, 10 cm (4 in) apart. This helps to support the dough weight when it is hung upside down. Now is a good time to work out how you will hang your panettone upside down. I often hang mine between two piles of books or between two chairs.

If you can't find panettone baking papers, feel free to use any round baking tin (lined with baking paper) to create a similar effect or simply bake in a well-oiled bread tin.

To make the white flour leaven, follow the feeding instructions below.

WHITE FLOUR LEAVEN

- 5 g (0.17 oz) wholemeal (whole-wheat) leaven (at 150% hydration)
- 150 g (5.3 oz) white bread flour
- 150 g (5.3 oz) water

Add the wholemeal leaven, bread flour and water to a clean jar and mix extremely well with a small spatula, checking there are no dry patches of flour at the base of the jar. This will make 305 g (10.7 oz) leaven.

Allow the leaven to reach full fermentation, reaching its maximum height and then letting it crash a little, before feeding. Use the two-rubber band method (see page 32) to help you keep track.

FIRST FEED

- Keep 50 g (1.76 oz)
- Discard 250 g (8.82 oz)
- Add 100 g (3.52 oz) white bread flour
- Add 130 g (4.58 oz) milk, at 35°C (95°F)

Complete the first feed, mixing well and ensuring there are no dry patches of flour at the base of the jar. This will produce 280 g (9.87 oz) milk leaven.

SECOND FEED

- Keep 50 g (1.76 oz)
- Discard 230 g (8.11 oz)
- Add 100 g (3.52 oz) white bread flour
- Add 130 g (4.58 oz) milk, at 35°C (95°F)

Complete the second feed, then continue to feed the leaven, using the second feed ingredients quantities, until the leaven fully ferments in 4 hours or less.

Meanwhile, make the fruit and liqueur mix 2 days before you make the panettone, to allow the fruits to fully macerate.

FRUIT & LIQUEUR MIX

- 180 g (6.35 oz) soft golden sultanas (golden raisins)
- peel of 1 orange, pith scraped away, peel very finely sliced
- juice of 1 orange, seeds removed
- 1¼ tablespoons vanilla extract
- 1 tablespoon honey
- 1 teaspoon Amaretto
- 1 tablespoon Cointreau
- 1 tablespoon Marsala

PANETTONE DOUGH

- 40 g (1.41 oz) full-cream (whole) milk
- 2 egg yolks
- 4 whole eggs
- 280 g (9.87 oz) white flour leaven, made with milk (see opposite), at 130% hydration
- 11 g (0.39 oz) salt
- 130 g (4.58 oz) caster (superfine) sugar
- 550 g (19.4 oz) white bread flour, plus extra for dusting
- 160 g (5.64 oz) cold butter, cut into small squares and left to soften slightly

Combine the fruit and liqueur ingredients in a small bowl, cover with a saucer and leave to macerate at room temperature. On the day you plan to make the panettone, strain any liquor not absorbed by the fruit and enjoy it with friends.

To make the panettone dough, add the milk, egg yolks, eggs, leaven, salt, sugar and flour to the bowl of a stand mixer with the dough hook attached. Mix on medium speed for 5 minutes, then reduce the speed to slow and add the butter, a cube at a time, until fully incorporated.

Cover the mixing bowl with a clean tea towel and allow the dough to rest for 30 minutes.

Knead the dough on medium speed for 15 minutes, making sure the dough doesn't exceed 30°C (86°F) (test the dough with a food thermometer halfway through mixing and allow it to rest if it gets too warm).

Cover the mixing bowl again and allow the dough to rest for 30 minutes. Repeat the 15-minute kneading and 30-minute resting process.

Knead the dough again for 15 minutes, then reduce the speed to slow and add the fruit in small batches, with the mixer running, to evenly distribute the fruit through the dough. Continue to knead for 1 minute. Alternatively laminate the dough (see page 124), adding most of the fruit to the first lamination layer. Distribute the remaining fruit among each lamination fold, as you bring the lamination back to a cohesive dough. This ensures none of the macerated fruit is squashed by the dough hook. As this is an onerous recipe, choose a pathway that allows you to enjoy the making of this delicious bread year after year.

Bulk ferment the dough by placing it in a lightly oiled transparent rectangular food container. Gently flatten the dough and mark its height on the container, then cover with the lid. Check the dough frequently until it has risen by one-third (see page 130).

Tip the dough out of the food container and onto your kitchen bench. Dust the surface of the dough lightly with flour, then flip the dough floured-side down. Stretch the dough out a little on all sides to create a 30 cm x 40 cm (12 in x 15¾ in) rectangle. Fold the right side of the dough into the centre, then fold the left side on top of the previous fold. Grab the end furthest away from you and fold it all the way down on top of the two first folds, then, finally, stretch the end closest to you and bring it up and away from you, to cover all the other folds. Roll the dough away from you so the seams are on the bottom of the dough. Now use the drag, rotate and tuck motion to tension the dough (see page 138).

Place the dough inside the prepared paper mould, on top of the metal skewers, and allow to proof in a warm place until the dough is billowy and has increased to almost double its original height. Use the poke test along the way to assess fermentation (see page 156).

Three-quarter fill a baking tray with water and place it on the floor of your oven.

Preheat the oven to 230°C (445°F).

Transfer the panettone to the oven and bake for 20 minutes. Reduce the temperature to 190°C (375°F) and continue to bake for about 30 minutes, until the internal temperature of the panettone reaches 95°C (203°F) on a food thermometer. If the top of the panettone seems to be darkening too much, place the panettone on a lower oven shelf and cover the top gently with an upturned baking tin.

Remove the panettone from the oven and use the skewers to hang it upside down for a few hours until it has cooled fully. The skewers will be extremely hot, so make sure they are out of reach of children and pets.

The panettone will keep in an airtight container in the fridge for up to 2 weeks. *Buon appetito!*

Acknowledgements

A big, gigantic, appreciative thank you to the following beautiful big-hearted people: Mamma Rita Ripani, Lise Temple, Ralf Pfleiderer, Ken Hercott, Paul Demchy, John Reid, Rachel Turner, Rachel Jelley, Amy Atkinson, Holly Watson-Reeves, Sam Westbrooke, Amber Stephens, Robyn Rogers, Ryan Andrijich, Penny Mansley, Lucy Heaver, Hannah Koelmeyer and Claire Rochford. Thank you for your help with the writing of this book and for creating spaces that allow not only for the fermentation of dough, but community too. Dreams only ever come true with the support of others – thank you a million trillion for helping me create this lovely paper book dream.

Index

Published in 2026 by Smith Street Books
Naarm (Melbourne) | Australia
smithstreetbooks.com

Distributed outside of ANZ, North & Latin America by Thames & Hudson Ltd.,
6–24 Britannia Street, London, WC1X 9JD | thamesandhudson.com

EU Authorised Representative: Interart S.A.R.L.
19 rue Charles Auray, 93500 Pantin, Paris, France
productsafety@thameshudson.co.uk; www.interart.fr

ISBN: 978-1-9232-3979-1

Smith Street Books respectfully acknowledges the Wurundjeri People of the Kulin Nation, who are the Traditional Owners of the land on which we work, and we pay our respects to their Elders past and present.

Publisher: Hannah Koelmeyer
Editor: Penny Mansley
Recipe editor: Lucy Heaver
Design, layout and illustrations: Claire Rochford
Photographer: Mara Ripani
Proofreader: Ariana Klepac
Indexer: Rachel Pitts
Prepress: Megan Ellis
Production manager: Aisling Coughlan

Printed & bound in China by C&C Offset Printing Co., Ltd.

Book 436
10 9 8 7 6 5 4 3 2 1